LOCKDOWN 2020
- A Moment in Time -

*Stories of love, hope and transformation
in a turbulent world*

•

Penny Plimmer & Martine Bolton

Copyright © 2020 Penny Plimmer & Martine Bolton.
ISBN: 978-1-8381634-2-6
Photography, © Penny Plimmer, Japics Photographic
Design and print origination, Tricia Charles, Charles Design Associates
Cover design, Richard Pegg

All rights reserved. No part of this work may be copied, photocopied, reproduced, translated or reduced to any electronic medium or machine-readable form, in whole or in part, without specific permission from the copyright owner or in accordance with the provisions of the Copyright, Designs and Patents Act 1988. Licences issued by the Copyright Licensing Agency Limited do not extend to this work. Distribution for commercial purposes is strictly prohibited.

Warning: The doing of an unauthorised act in relation to a copyright work may result in both a civil claim for damages and criminal prosecution.
The authors have made every effort to trace all copyright holders, but if any has been inadvertently overlooked we would be pleased to make the necessary arrangement at the first opportunity.
Printed by Pulsio Print UK

This book is dedicated to the amazing people and organisations whose stories feature within it, and to the everyday superheroes all around the world who went 'above and beyond the call of duty' to support their friends, families, neighbours and communities through the difficult lockdown period.
It is also dedicated to Penny's sons, Ben and William Plimmer, and to her grandson, Maxwell.

We honour, celebrate and salute you!

CONTENTS

About This Book	1
Community Stories	3
Charity Stories	23
NHS & Key Worker Stories	41
Business Stories	57
Entertainment Stories	91
Creativity Stories	109
Transformation Stories	123
Miscellaneous Stories	137
Epilogue	154
Acknowledgements	155

ABOUT THIS BOOK

Hello, and thank you for choosing to pick up this book. As its creators, we (commercial photographer, Penny Plimmer, and personal development consultant and author, Martine Bolton) hope you will feel as moved, inspired and uplifted reading it, as we have felt in compiling it.

In early May 2020, an innocent little conversation between the two us sparked an idea, which became a project, which resulted in the book in front of you. At that point, the UK had been in full lockdown for about six weeks in response to the coronavirus SARS-CoV-2 which was causing Covid-19 – an infectious disease affecting the respiratory system. Work for both of us, as freelancers, had largely come to a halt at that time.

Penny mentioned the doorstep photography she'd been doing whilst out for her daily lockdown exercise. She'd been taking photos of people and families in front of their homes, along with the colourful rainbow art and teddy bears that were springing up in windows everywhere. I (Martine) responded that I could imagine the photos in an art gallery exhibition, and as a large, coffee-table book with personal stories accompanying the photographs. Penny loved the idea, and so we agreed to work together to bring it to life.

We recognised that we were living through an historic moment in time, and wanted to tell the story of what happened in our region from the human perspective. As awful as the situation was, we could see a lot of great things happening too, and we recognised the potential for something good to come out of it. Nobody else seemed to be doing it locally, and we believed we could do the job justice. It became our 'passion project'!

We had no idea at that stage how we would finance it, or make it all happen. I had written and released another book at the end of 2019, but that was a personal development book – a very different kind of proposal, and whilst I'd done a few talks and signings in the ensuing months, all that was shelved when the virus hit.

We had time on our hands, if not money, and were both of the mindset that if you really want to do something, you shouldn't worry too much about how you'll make it happen – just make a start, and the rest will follow. It was a leap of faith, and more work that we'd imagined. Our initial idea of a collection of 30-40 stories became over 60 in the end, but we believe they all have a place.

We hope you will love the book, and treasure it for years to come!
Martine & Penny xx

COMMUNITY STORIES

One of the most heartening things to witness during the *Covid-19* pandemic was the huge resurgence in community spirit and kindness that took place.

On 16th March, a week before the formal lockdown was announced, Health Secretary Matt Hancock advised the public against all unnecessary social contact and travel, particularly for those over 70, pregnant or with underlying health conditions.

University lecturer Becky Wass from Falmouth in Cornwall made the news when she designed a postcard for people wanting to volunteer their help to self-isolating neighbours. The BBC posted a 'print-at-home' copy of the postcard on their website for people to complete and post through neighbours' letterboxes, and this went viral.

Some streets and communities set up *Facebook* and *WhatsApp* groups, where people could offer their help, or ask for things that they needed.

Community organisations did amazing work in identifying those who needed extra support, and in recruiting volunteers to help.

The phrase "We're all in this together" became commonplace, and despite the social distancing that we were asked to do, the crisis seemed to bring us closer together in many cases – emotionally, at least. From a world where many of us had centred our lives around ourselves and our families, our awareness of the wider community seemed to expand, and we became more thoughtful, kind and considerate of others – a generalisation, of course, but true of many.

Globalisation, for all its benefits, had enabled the rapid spread of the virus, and exposed the weakness in lengthy supply chains. Where the super-markets struggled to get hold of stock in the early days of lockdown, the smaller, independent community stores which rely on local suppliers and growers, fared much better. Shopping and eating 'local' were no longer just ethically fashionable ways of meeting our consumption needs, they became a necessity – for some items at least. We were being forced into changing our habits.

According to UK charity *The Mental Health Foundation*, people who are more socially connected to family, friends, and/or their community are happier and live longer, healthier lives with fewer physical and mental health problems than those who are less well connected. Like ants or bees, humans are hardwired for community living, and need quality connection in order to thrive in our world.

We hope you will enjoy these stories of community, and perhaps be inspired to connect with others at a deeper level - even once the virus has gone.

01 Adrian Segovia

Adrian Segovia is the postmaster at *Waltham Chase Post Office*. Originally from Gibraltar, he came to the UK in 1991 at the age of 18. For many years he worked in casinos all around the world, including London, Bournemouth, the US, Australia, New Orleans and Southampton, before throwing his hand in during 2011, for life in rural Hampshire.

Adrian has been running the post office and shop at Waltham Chase ever since, along with his wife Jenny, and has hardly missed a day's work. Open seven days a week, he generally takes one holiday day a year (on Christmas day), although this increased to a day and a half in the year he got married! Christmases and wedding days aside, he hasn't taken a proper holiday in nine years, although he was due to take his six-year-old youngest daughter to Gibraltar on 4th April, to meet his wider family for the first time. When the country went into lockdown a couple of weeks beforehand, the plans sadly had to be cancelled.

Post office life is busy at the best of times, and can be physically and mentally exhausting. Adrian is generally up at 6am, and regularly works until midnight. Lockdown saw him busier than ever, as he did everything he could to keep his customers supplied with the essentials.

A sufferer of chronic bronchitis, Adrian should really have been shielding himself. However, there was a hungry village to serve, and he's just not the kind of person to sit around and do nothing. He described the early lockdown period as "absolute chaos". The supermarkets were struggling with supplies, and many people were turning to their local independent shops instead. Where the shop would normally have sold around 12 crates of eggs a week, they were selling 12 in a day. Where they would normally have sold around 40 loaves of bread a week, they were selling easily 70 a day.

The shop adopted a 'One in, one out' system from the start, and customers appreciated it. Safety was key, and people started to come from further afield because they'd heard of the system, and felt more comfortable shopping that way.

A sufferer of chronic bronchitis, Adrian should really have been shielding himself. However, there was a hungry village to serve, and he's just not the kind of person to sit around and do nothing.

Trying to manage the panic buying taking place in the early days was difficult, and Adrian had to have some difficult conversations with customers. With an eye on the wider community, and ensuring everyone got what they needed, he had to ration the sale of certain items rather than allow stockpiling. Some customers were coming in multiple times a day, and sending in different family members to double or triple up on items, and he had to try and deal with these situations as best he could, in the interests of the wider community.

In some ways, the lack of supply reminded Adrian of his early life in Gibraltar. In the late 1960s, General Franco closed the border with Spain, halting the supply of good. Most items had to be shipped over from Morocco, and sometimes shipments wouldn't come through, meaning stock would be unavailable. It was a close-knit community where people knew and helped each other; where they would rarely lock their homes, and would often leave the keys in their cars. People were honest, loyal and trustworthy.

"Going above and beyond the call of duty" is a phrase that's often overused, but in the case of Adrian, Jenny and their team of helpers, it's exactly what they did. They'd always used local suppliers for their stock wherever possible, and this really worked in their favour during the lockdown. When few places were able to source bread, flour and pasta, they were usually able to find some through their local contacts. During the height of the virus Adrian was continuously in motion, and regularly stayed up until 3am talking to suppliers. Somehow, he managed to keep going.

They ran a delivery service during this time covering not just Waltham Chase, but also neighbouring villages such as Botley, Shirrell Heath, Swanmore and Bishops Waltham. They had a list of customers whom they would text regularly for delivery orders, and a team of seven people on delivery service. They even opened up out of hours for some customers who were unable (or afraid) to shop during normal opening hours.

It took the pandemic for many people to realise how much our post offices and local shops do for their customers. For some people in the community, a trip to the post office might be the only contact they have with life outside of their homes, and it can truly be a lifeline.

What Adrian and Jenny did over lockdown is not much different from what they've always done – they just helped more people over a wider area, working longer hours. As restrictions slowly started to ease, and life returned to some semblance of 'normal', some customer stayed with them, and others went back to the big supermarkets. Adrian just hopes that people will remember that the little shops are there all year around. Without them, some people might not survive.

Adrian is thrilled to have received a lot of recognition for his hard work and dedication this year, having been nominated for a number of different awards and honours. His three daughters are very proud of their daddy, and his youngest is hoping he'll get to meet The Queen one day!

We can't think of anyone who deserves the honour more!

02 Janet Ayers

Janet Ayres is a vocal practitioner, community artist, non-religious celebrant and performer who lives in Southsea. She's also leader of the *Southsea Community Choir* – a natural voice choir, open to all, who sing for fun and performance at various local concerts and festivals, raising money for charities including *Water Aid*.

The choir sings songs from all over the world, including folk songs, blues, peace songs, protest songs, and more - some in different languages. There are physical actions that accompany some of the songs too, so it's a fully embodied and multisensory experience.

When the country went into lockdown, Janet took her choir (who normally meet in person on Tuesday evenings at *Trinity Methodist Church* in Southsea) online, via video-conferencing platform *Zoom*. She knew it would be important for her choir members to continue their regular practice, and whilst some members weren't sure about moving online to start with, in the end, most were able to embrace it.

Janet would begin with a vocal warm-up on Facebook Live, and then transfer onto Zoom afterwards for the choir practice session, where members could see each other and interact a bit more. She would send out different documents and files to the choir members each week for them to practise and learn between the online meetings. Then, they would all come together to sing their parts collectively on *Zoom* – albeit with microphones muted because of time-delay problems! Mics were then un-muted between songs, so that everyone could have a chat and a giggle. It was gloriously chaotic, but worked in its own crazy way.

A community choir may, on the surface, appear to be all about music and singing. Scratch the surface though, and what you'll find underneath is much deeper in meaning, and has multiple benefits. The *Southsea Community Choir* is about fun, friendship, connection, unity, well-being (body, mind and spirit), learning, and even healing. Music – and singing in particular - has a profound effect on every cell in the body, and can measurably uplift us and keep us happy and healthy. The biggest benefits are realised when we actively participate, rather than just listen.

Learning to sing new songs is really good for the brain, and Janet also runs dementia-friendly singing groups, along with the 'Hayling Huffers' – a group for people with lung disease, as singing strengthens muscles and improves breathing co-ordination too.

Aside from the choir, Janet also sings solo, and has performed at two funerals this year. One was an outdoor burial with a few family members present, where she sang 'All Things Bright & Beautiful' and 'I Watch the Sunrise'. The other was a crematorium funeral, where she sang 'Amazing Grace'. She also sang and played the violin via *Zoom* for a friend's father on a couple of occasions, to lift his spirits whilst he was at home in between cancer treatments.

Janet also performs as part of a duo with her partner Matt Parsons, who plays the banjolele. They usually do a lot of performances within care homes, but whilst they were able to do a few garden concerts this year, most of their gigs were cancelled due to the virus.

But music isn't the only good thing in life! Food became even more important to people during lockdown, and Janet found herself baking a lot of apple cakes and cheese scones. She would put a post on her *Facebook* page when she'd baked a batch asking if anyone wanted some, and would enjoy the walk and doorstep chats afterwards as she hand-delivered them.

> *The Southsea Community Choir is about fun, friendship, connection, unity, well-being (body, mind and spirit), learning, and even healing.*

Janet is also a trainer illustrator, and has been awarded an honorary degree from the *University of Portsmouth* for her community music and art work. She was due to attend a formal ceremony in July, which had to be postponed until May 2021. In fact, there's a lot that Janet's looking forward to in 2021, including the time when the choir can get back together again in person; when concerts and festivals are back on the agenda; and when she can run art workshops again, such as the 'Drawing for Well-being' classes that she's run previously for the *Good Mental Health Cooperative*.

Thank you, Janet, for continuing to uplift your community with music, food, fun and friendship, even through these difficult times.

Janet can be contacted via the *Natural Voice Network*: www.naturalvoice.net/practitioner/janetayers

03 Jan Orme

Jan Orme is a business trainer and former English teacher who lives in Hamble-le-Rice. She kept herself very busy during the lockdown period by helping the people in her village.

Here are just a few of the ways in which she helped:
- She went shopping for people and delivered newspapers, the local parish magazine, flowers, bulbs, and so on.
- She paid doorstep/garden visits to people that live on their own, to check in with them and have a friendly chat.
- She took lemon drizzle cake around to neighbours on Thursday afternoons.
- She also compiled two short memoirs, 'Lessons I've learnt from lockdown' and 'Lessons from letterboxes', following her many interesting jaunts around the village, having never realised there were quite so many different letterbox varieties!

Jan feels that she's learnt so much from lockdown, and has felt very humbled at times - often shedding a few tears whilst out on her rounds, thinking about how brave and amazing everyone's been.

She's also been touched at how grateful the village's residents have been, thanking her with all sorts of gifts, including chocolates, wine, flowers, eggs, and other things. She feels that she got so much out of helping people, that she should be the one thanking them – not the other way around!

Many thanks Jan, for all you've done to help your community through the lockdown period.

Lessons learnt from lockdown … so far …

I have learnt how:
- proud
- independent
- fearful
- courageous
- brave

our 'elderly & vulnerable' people are.

I have learnt how difficult, therefore, it must have been for them to put their hands up and say they needed help.

I have learnt how trust grows and develops. People give their shopping lists; letters to post; parcels to return. They worry how they will pay. They give a 'kitty'; a bank card; money on the doorstep – never wanting to be in debt to you.

I have learnt how those who didn't 'formally' volunteer, have stepped up and acted as kind, concerned and caring neighbours. They look out for people around them who may need some help – shopping, meals, phone calls – to help curb their loneliness.

I have learnt how grateful these people are, for small acts of kindness, that cost nothing.

I have learnt not to take things for granted – like jumping in the car to go here, there and everywhere for shopping and driving to Lee-on-the-Solent to have a coffee and a wonderful walk along the Promenade.

I have even learnt that getting on the 6:03 am in to London Waterloo, boarding crowded buses or tube trains to just go to work – may be a thing of the past.

I have learnt to say (when people thank me for doing shopping, picking up a paper, buying stamps or dropping off a parcel) "no, thank you".

Thank you for:
- staying indoors
- doing as you've been told by the Government
- giving up your independence
- relying on others
- foregoing the hobbies you share with others
- not visiting the clubs you so much enjoy
- giving up the activities which added value to your lives.·
- foregoing the hobbies you share with others
- not visiting the clubs you so much enjoy
- giving up the activities which added value to your lives.

Thank you for playing such a key part in protecting us, your neighbours in Hamble. You've totally supported the NHS and have helped stop this virus. It has been – and will continue to be, a pleasure and a privilege to be there for you for as long as necessary.

04

Bishop Waltham Rotary Club

A Rotary Club is a group of individuals united in the spirit of humanitarian service to the community and wider world, through commitment, compassion, skill sharing, professionalism and fun.

Bishops Waltham has a particularly active club that organises the annual carnival and show, as well as running a fund-raising stall at the annual Christmas fayre, and transporting *Santa* and his elves around the local area on 'Roger the Christmas Train'.

The club had a number of fundraising events lined up for 2020, including the carnival, a fashion show and a 'Tour of Legends'. Disappointingly, it all had to be cancelled when the country went into lockdown, hence the club lost their main means of fundraising.

Many of their members were in the 'vulnerable' category, either shielding loved ones or self-isolating. Weekly face-to-face meetings became fortnightly and online, with some members having to be trained in a few technical skills.

A weekly quiz was held on *Zoom*, as well as monthly council meetings to address requests for help (Rotary has its own charity, with one of its key aims being eradicating polio).

Although the club's fundraising was down, members were still able to help various causes in different ways, including:
- Purchasing two *Chromebooks* for a local school to assist home-schooling children
- Donating TVs to Winchester Hospital for Covid isolation room patient
- Donating money to start a hot food, home-delivery lunch service to local residents
- Assisting local food banks and a local school with food, in particular for families finding it difficult at this time
- Helping the *Bishops Waltham Emergency Response Team* with deliveries, and acting as *Street Ambassadors* in the High Street.

Club members don't know when they'll be able to meet again face-to-face, but will continue to do all they can in the spirit of service, no matter what.

True to their website's banner, they are people of action, making a difference in their community. Very inspiring!

05 Livtar Kaur

Livtar Kaur is a former primary academy chief executive officer (CEO) turned yoga teacher, trainer and vegan/raw chef. She runs yoga classes, retreats and cookery workshops from her business in Alverstoke – Sushmuna Yoga, Vegan & Raw Food.

Seva, in yoga, is the concept of selfless service, and Langar is the practice of freely sharing food with others. When the country first went into lockdown, Livtar had plenty of chapatti and bread flour in stock, ready for a workshop. Residents of the road where she lives had set up a *WhatsApp* group, and were commenting that they were struggling to buy bread and/or flour, and so Livtar decided to bake some loaves, and put them on her wall for people to collect.

The bread went very quickly, and people started asking for more, and placing orders. Livtar was able to source more flour from a friend, and would put a post in the *WhatsApp* group inviting orders whenever she was baking, which she later delivered to people's doorsteps.

She also made cakes, biscuits and chocolates for people when she knew of birthdays coming up. All were given freely and received gratefully, with the option of making donations to the NHS.

One resident opened up his driveway to neighbours, naming it 'Bar 36', for everyone to help celebrate another neighbour and his wife's birthdays, where everyone enjoyed a socially-distanced drink and piece of cake together!

One resident opened up his driveway to neighbours, naming it 'Bar36', for everyone to help celebrate another neighbour and his wife's birthdays, where everyone enjoyed a socially-distanced drink and piece of cake together!

Livtar found the community spirit between her neighbours to be excellent, with people helping each other in all manner of ways. Some residents were feeling rather anxious and confused at the start of lockdown, but the community spirit that was shared enabled them to feel more connected and supported.

On the final night of the customary Thursday evening 'Clap for our Carers' (more on the origins of this in the 'NHS & Key Worker Stories' section of the book), the neighbours all pledged to start a new tradition of coming out of their homes and waving to each other instead!

Thank you for your kindness, Livtar, and inspiring us with the practices of Seva and Langar.

Terry & Robbie Cattermole

Terry Cattermole is a retired Royal Navy weapons specialist, and his wife Robbie has a background in amateur theatre, having been an actress, costume designer and director.

The couple are now retired, and live full and active lives volunteering for a number of different organisations, and being members of the award-winning drama company, *Southsea Shakespeare Actors*.

Terry and Robbie returned to the UK in 2015, having lived in the town of Duras in south-western France for 25 years – the smallest 'appellation contrôlée' wine region in the country, some 60 miles from Bordeaux. During their time in the town, the couple were made honorary citizens, with Terry receiving the additional honour of 'Chevalier'. Amusingly, from their home in Marmion Avenue, Southsea, they are just 210 metres or so from their local branch of Waitrose, where they can sometimes find a nice bottle of *Côtes de Duras*!

The couple now live in Marmion Avenue in Southsea. The name holds a special meaning for Terry, as *HMS Marmion* was an Algerine-class minesweeper which served with distinction during World War II. Terry served on board her sister-ship *HMS Wave* in the late 1950s.

When the country went into lockdown in March 2020, most of the couple's usual commitments and activities stopped. Never ones to be idle, they kept themselves busy with a variety of projects around the home, multiple walks on Southsea's seafront and common, and by staying in touch with their friends and family.

Earlier in the year, one of the couple's younger neighbours, Sarah, had suggested holding a street party to celebrate the 75th anniversary of *Victory in Europe (VE) Day*. Terry and Robbie thought this was an excellent idea, as Marmion Avenue is a quiet little no-through road, and would be perfect for such an event. The neighbours all agreed, Council permission was sought, and the 'go-ahead' was given.

Plans for the event took shape, and then disaster hit in the form of Covid-19. It seemed that a wonderful opportunity to celebrate a momentous event (and share time in the company of other 'Marmioneers'), might be going down the tubes. However, after discussions and consultations, the consensus was that the event should still go ahead, with some modifications.

Bunting and flags were put up in preparation for the big day, and a socially distanced tea-party took place starting in the late morning, running into the afternoon and then extending into the evening, when a few alcoholic beverages were consumed!

It was a great opportunity for the residents of the flats to get to know those who live in the nearby cottages better, and to elevate relationships from a nodding and greeting basis to first-name terms.

Sometime in the evening, and as the event had been such a success, one of the residents suggested they do something similar on a weekly basis. Thus, the 'Friday Evening Wine O'Clock Club' was born, and was still going strong at the time of publishing (November 2020). Residents meet up at 5:30 pm in the forecourt of the flats when the weather's fine, and in the hallway when it's not, with a socially distanced glass in hand – helping to keep sales of wine at the local Waitrose buoyant!

Sometime in the evening, and as the event had been such a success, one of the residents suggested they do something similar on a weekly basis. Thus, the 'Friday Evening Wine O'Clock Club' was born ...

Terry and Robbie have kept in good cheer throughout lockdown, staying in touch with their friends and family, safely socialising with their neighbours, and taking in the fresh sea air where they live. They're looking forward to the time when an effective vaccine against the virus is available worldwide, so that public health and the economy can get back on track, and they can return to their voluntary work and activities once again.

We'll raise a glass to that, Terry and Robbie. "Santé!".

07 Ayesha Hussain

Ayesha Hussain is a former housing support officer from Southampton who owns office cleaning company *Loyalty Clean*, covering the Portsmouth, Fareham and Southampton areas.

During lockdown, Ayesha's next-door neighbour Sophie – a retired school teacher – had a fall. She was 87 years old, and had been ill for around eight months. Sophie deteriorated rapidly towards the end, experiencing dramatic weight-loss, but she didn't like visiting doctors or hospitals, and didn't want to see a specialist. Unable to keep any food down, she'd grown so weak that she collapsed on her doorstep one day. Neighbours had taken her back in to the house, settled her onto the sofa, and called for an ambulance. As the paramedics couldn't find anything obviously wrong with her, and because she didn't want to go into hospital, they left again, asking neighbours to call in and keep an eye on her periodically.

> *During her ill-health, an array of friends and neighbours, including Ayesha, had come together to help Sophie with her with shopping, gardening, errands, bills, cleaning, and taking her to appointments.*

Sophie was someone that didn't like to ask for help, and had no living relatives in the UK. She was a very kind person who cared about the community, loved children and animals, and especially loved her cat Daisy, who she fed on a diet of fresh chicken. During her ill-health, an array of friends and neighbours, including Ayesha, had come together to help Sophie with her with shopping, gardening, errands, bills, cleaning, and taking her to appointments. In fact, residents of the road where they all live came together more than ever before during lockdown, getting to know one another better, looking out for each another, and helping each other through an array of accidents, incidents and ordeals.

On the 1st April at 2:10 am, Sophie passed away. Ayesha had sat with her for the preceding 15 hours, as the doctor had advised there was no need to worry about the potential risk of virus transmission, as Sophie was unlikely to live much longer. She wasn't speaking during this time, and her eyes had become fixed. Feeling unsure what to do, Ayesha called Keith, a long-term friend of Sophie's, and he came over and joined her. The pair stayed with Sophie until she passed away, at which point Ayesha's husband took over the vigil until the undertaker arrived.

Ayesha and the neighbourhood community that had come together to help Sophie through her difficult last few months were desperately sad to see her go, but felt thankful that they'd been able to be there for her towards the end. After a bit of a fight, Daisy the cat went back to the Blue Cross rehoming centre where she'd come from. The pair's absence has left a big void.

Nothing lasts for ever, and life has to go on, but this wonderful group of neighbours won't forget their friend in a hurry. They will always remember lockdown as a time of highs and lows, but one where the glue that holds a community together became stronger, through their collective and loving support of one lovely lady.

08 Jason Rule

Jason Rule is a retired builder (and man of many talents), from Southampton. He and his wife Sue took early retirement a number of years ago, and have never been busier – particularly this year.

The list of projects and activities that Jason tackled during lockdown is enough to take anyone's breath away. They include (but are not limited to):

- Regular shopping and food deliveries for four different households.

- Making bread for friends and neighbours – a new skill for Jason. A friend was able to supply large sacks of flour when the supermarkets' supply had dried up, so Jason decided to give bread-making a go. After a few failures, he learnt how to make a decent loaf, and having found his stride, he got a weekly flow going.
- He learned how to use *Zoom*, and ran lots of online quizzes for friends and the Rotary group he belongs to – many of whom were sceptical about video-linking initially, but came to embrace the idea, and eagerly looked forward to it each week.
- He renovated, repaired and improved his home to an extent he'd never have managed, had it not been for lockdown.
- He started to build a new house on the plot he'd bought next door to his own home. He bought a digger when the contractors he'd booked to landscape the ground weren't able to work, and ended up doing lots of jobs for neighbours who were keen to level their ground, remove their hedging and pull up old tree stumps, etc. He also learnt how to weld in order to make reinforcement cages for the concrete.
- He did lots of restoration work on his two classic cars.
- He whittled a number of items out of wood in his workshop, and learned to make hurdle fencing out of hazel from a nearby wood. He also made disability aids for a close, and formerly very fit, active friend who developed Progressive Multifocal Leukoencephalopathy (PML), leaving him bed bound. He also made a croquet set, and learned how to play using the proper rules, after finding out it was a very different game to what he'd thought.
- He walked "for no apparent reason" (his own words) with his wife, Sue – something she'd always really enjoyed, but he'd never personally understood! He still doesn't really understand why people walk for pleasure, and likes things to have an end goal or purpose!

Jason clearly loves to keep busy, and admitted he never finds the time to sit around, or read a book – even when on holiday.

He enjoyed getting to know neighbours of over 20 years that he'd previously only been on nodding terms with, and found them all to be (his own words again) "quite nice after all"! This stemmed from going outside on Thursday evenings to clap for the carers, and also from creating a 'Neighbourhood Watch' style *WhatsApp* group.

> *He enjoyed getting to know neighbours of over 20 years that he'd previously only been on nodding terms with, and found them all to be (his own words again) "quite nice after all"!*

As a member of *Bishop Waltham's Rotary Club*, Jason enjoys working and playing with his fellow Rotarians to raise money for charity and give something back to society. All of their usual spring/summer events (fetes, classic car runs, fashion shows, and so on) had to be cancelled during lockdown. The club typically raises around £25,000 a year, and Jason hopes they'll find a way of replacing the lost income somehow.

On a sad note he lost two friends to the virus, and found attending their funerals to be a very strange experience, with limited numbers. Friends of theirs, who they'd spent many holidays with when their respective children were growing up, tragically lost their bright and beautiful 24-year-old daughter to cancer. Bereavement can be a lonely time in any circumstances, but the isolation of lockdown no doubt made it more difficult for some.

2020 was a year that gave, and one that also took away. It's a year that Jason won't forget in a hurry.

Fiona Leow

Fiona Loew is a mother of six from Southsea with a number of health issues including chronic fatigue, fibromyalgia and high blood pressure. She has good days and bad days, when her symptoms can be very severe. Being considered disabled, she was advised by her doctor to stay home when the virus hit the UK.

Fiona's husband works for a bank in Lombardy in northern Italy, usually coming back to the UK one weekend a month, and one week every three months. Lombardy (the centre of a massive outbreak of the virus) went into complete lockdown in February. Fiona hadn't seen her husband since Christmas, but with two of her children still living at home, she wasn't on her own.

As a keen seamstress and crafter, Fiona decided that she needed to do something to keep herself busy on the days that she felt well enough. Having a good stash of fabric to hand, she set about making protective facemasks – initially for family and friends, but later on deciding to scale up and start producing more.

A friend told her about a *Facebook* group called 'Community Mask Trees' where people were making facemasks and hanging them from trees for others to take. According to the group, there are at least 160 community mask trees throughout the country (and probably many more), and Fiona decided she would help her community by creating one for the Southsea area.

Having a good stash of fabric to hand, she set about making protective facemasks – initially for family and friends, but later on deciding to scale up and start producing more.

To date, she's made over 700 masks, which take about an hour each when you include the cutting and pinning (which she does in bed) and the sewing, which she does on her machine when she's having good days. She leaves the masks on a wooden 'tree' made by her son, by the front gate of her home in Winter Road. People can then help themselves, leaving a suggested donation of £2 if they're able, to cover the cost of materials. Fiona intends to keep making the masks for as long as there's a need, on the days that she's able.

Fiona used to run a crafting group for home-schooled children, as her own children were home-schooled too. She would like to set up a new group for all ages once it's safe to do so.

In terms of the future, she's looking forward to seeing her husband again soon, as well as her daughter, who lives and works in London.

Thank you so much Fiona for devoting your time and energy to making these masks. You may never know how many lives you've helped to save, but we feel sure that your community will always be thankful for what you've done to protect them.

CHARITY STORIES

Charities had an interesting ride in 2020. Whilst one-off donations to the *goDonate* platform (covering charities such as *NSPCC*, *Prostate Cancer UK*, *Stroke Association*, *The Firefighters Charity* and *Battersea Dogs' & Cats' Home*) reportedly went up by over 560% in April, May and June compared to the same period the previous year, some charities reported facing bankruptcy due to event cancellations/lost fundraising income, and soaring demand for their services.

Captain Sir Tom Moore famously raised nearly £33 million for NHS Charities Together in the run-up to his 100th birthday, by walking 100 laps of his garden. People in general seemed to become more giving and altruistic during the pandemic, with a number of high-profile celebrities including *Oprah Winfrey*, *Ariana Grande*, *Angelina Jolie*, *Rihanna*, *Lady Gaga*, *Elton John*, *Beyonce*, *George Clooney*, *Roger Federer*, *Arnold Schwarzenegger*, rock band *U2* and others hitting the news headlines after donating large sums to Covid-related causes. Other celebrities such as *Taylor Swift, Britney Spears* and *Miley Cyrus*, made more personal donations to specific individuals, families and organisations, to help them out din various circumstances.

Crowdfunding became a popular way for small businesses to seek donations and stay afloat during the lockdown, with the BBC reporting in April that funding website *GoFundMe* had seen a 246% increase in British business campaigns, on the same period the previous year.

The statistics on giving are interesting. The *UK Giving 2019* report highlighted that over 50% of those surveyed had given to charity in the previous year – 65% if you take sponsorship into account. The report also found that the over 50s are more generous than the under 50s; the over 75s give the most; charities supporting children/young people and animals are the best supported; women engage more than men, in terms of donating and volunteering; and the under 25s volunteer the most.

Research carried out at the *University of Manchester* demonstrated that the poorest in society give more generously than the rich do, as a percentage of income.

There are deep psychological principles involved in giving. When we give our time, money or energy to help others, we experience a profound sense of our own value. In helping others, we help ourselves too. It makes us feel good. We are rewarded with a release of dopamine known as the 'Helper's High' that gives us the feeling of a warm glow. It also seems that kindness is contagious. Dr David R Hamilton PhD quotes a contagion equation of $5 \times 5 \times 5 = 125$ in relation to acts of kindness: one act of kindness will inspire the recipient to carry out acts of kindness towards an average of five other people, who in turn will be kind towards five others, who will do the same. Before we know it, one simple act of kindness will have turned into 125 acts – much more contagious than Covid-19!

We hope the following stories from charities and charitable organisations will inspire you, and give you a warm glow!

10 Helping Hands – Bev Saunders

Bev Saunders is the founder of Helping Hands, Portsmouth – a charitable organisation with around 10 volunteers that's been reaching out to homeless and vulnerable people in Portsmouth since 2016.

The team go out delivering breakfasts on Mondays, Wednesdays and Fridays, and a cooked dinner and goodie bag on Sunday evenings, come rain, shine or snow. It is freshly home-made food, made with love and paid for out of the charitable donations they receive from the public. The service provided is not just about the food though – it's also about care, support, help in all forms, and kindness.

Bev continued with this amazing service all through the lockdown period, and didn't hold back on her trademark hugs. Gloved, masked and following stringent hygiene protocols, it was 'Business as Usual' for this dedicated superhero who the homeless community have come to know as 'Mum'.

To Bev's knowledge, none of Portsmouth's homeless contracted the virus, although a few individuals were housed in local hotels temporarily, and numbers were a bit down on usual. Some admitted to feeling scared and forgotten in the early stages of lockdown, believing that the help (outside of Helping Hands) just wasn't there for them during this difficult time.

Bev was grateful for the goodwill of Helping Hands' supporters throughout lockdown, many of whom were very generous in donating food items and doing shopping. She was particularly thankful to her local branch of ASDA for everything they did to assist the organisation.

The Helping Hands team relies on donations and public generosity to fund this work. They gratefully accept help of all kinds, and hope to be able to continue their service long into the future.

Bev believes that when a community works together, nobody needs to be cold, isolated or hungry.

Thank you, Bev and team, for everything you do towards this vision.

Anyone wanting more information, or to help, can go to Helping Hands' website: www.hhportsmouth.wordpress.com or join their *Facebook* group: www.facebook.com/groups/453845911452466/

11 Pompey in the Community - Clare Martin

Clare Martin is the CEO of Pompey in the Community – an independent charitable trust affiliated to *Portsmouth Football Club*. They offer sports and coaching, holiday clubs, before and after school clubs, lunchtime clubs, *National Citizen Service* (NCS) programmes, community cohesion, and health and educational programmes up to degree level, for people from all walks of life, aged two to 102.

When the country first went into lockdown, most of the organisation's staff were furloughed. Clare had submitted a proposal to *Portsmouth City Council* for the delivery of food parcels for those in vulnerable groups.

When *HIVE Portsmouth* (the city's official community hub, and 'First Response' coordination team during the pandemic) needed volunteers, many of Pompey in the Community's staff – including most of the football club's first team players – volunteered their services.

It was disappointing at the time to hear footballers generally receiving a bad press, as players around the country do a lot of charity work in their communities which goes unreported. In Pompey's case, the players almost all helped out, preparing, cooking and delivering meals along with other staff members.

Their whole facility became a warehouse during lockdown for food storage and meal production, as they worked with fellow charity *Enable Ability* to cook 80 hot meals a day, delivering between 400-500 food parcels a week at the peak of the virus, with a fleet of seven vans.

Clare was impressed with the way many of the businesses and organisations around the city came together to support people in the community. Many hotels, restaurants and ferry companies generously donated food, including a large number of Easter eggs. *The Queens Hotel* in Southsea and food manufacturer *Quattro Foods* both cooked a high volume of meals for distribution. It was a well-coordinated effort, helped along by generous grants from the *Department for Environment, Food and Rural Affairs* (DEFRA) and *Barclays Bank*.

As spring turned into summer, some of the organisation's usual activities began to return. *The National Citizen Service* (NCS) programme went ahead, albeit non-residential and with some restrictions, and the summer holiday clubs also took place, following similar guidelines to schools.

Personally, Clare had never been as busy as she was during lockdown. As well as overseeing all of this, and generally trying to keep funds coming in, she was also preparing funding bids for their big capital project to create a new community sports facility and hub, to be known as the *John Jenkins Stadium*. All going to plan, this will be based at the current *Moneyfields FC* site in the middle of the city, and will include two full-size 3G all-weather pitches, a multi-use games area, a training gym, a boxing gym, classrooms, a dance studio and a social club, amongst other facilities.

Clare is immensely proud of her team and of the city, and feels privileged to have been in a position to be able to help the community during the lockdown.

Looking ahead, she can't wait for the day when they can have their full complement of services back up and running again. They've been unable to continue the activities they usually run for their elderly and disabled customers, and Clare has missed seeing everyone. She believes there's nothing quite like face-to-face interaction, and has found it strange and difficult not being able to hug people, shake hands, and so on.

She's also looking forward to getting the new facility project over the line, helping to improve the lives and opportunities of even more local people.

Many hotels, restaurants and ferry companies generously donated food, including a large number of Easter eggs.

Many thanks to Clare and the team for the amazing work that they do all year around to benefit people of all kinds and all ages, and for their sterling efforts during the pandemic. We wish them all the best going forwards, and for the new stadium.

Pompey in the Community are always looking for volunteers and sponsors. Anyone wishing to help should email: info@pompeyitc.org.uk .

12 Music Fusion – Jinx Prowse

Jinx Prowse is the CEO of Music Fusion – a music charity comprising a young-person-friendly rehearsal space and recording studio in Havant, near Portsmouth.

The charity's aim is to provide a safe and creative space for young people aged 11-25 to connect, socialise and make great music.

The team specialises in working with young people experiencing challenging life circumstances such as serious mental health problems, social deprivation and being at risk of turning to crime, encouraging them to use their music as a platform for positive social action.

When lockdown was announced, they were in the middle of recording an album called 'Words Not Weapons / Mavericks 3'. It quickly became clear that some of their young people had begun to slide into dark and dangerous states of mind, so music leader Matt 'Blessed' Stevens came up with the idea of building a 'Recording Studio in a Box', which they could deliver to the homes of the young people to use.

The box was designed and developed, and the first to benefit was Kieran, whose mood and well-being had dropped so rapidly when lockdown was imposed, he was on the verge of suicide. The team immediately realised that he needed the outlet of channelling his thoughts and feelings into music, and were able to set him up remotely with a top producer to achieve a high-quality recording which later became part of the album.

To the team's surprise, when they went to collect the equipment, Kieran had also recorded and produced his own 4 track E.P. This was the equivalent, had the studio been open, of a music leader finishing a session, going home and coming in the next day to find the young person had stayed there all night and produced a ton of material! It showed a level of engagement and learning that surpassed the norm, and demonstrated what could be done with a captive audience! The mobile studio had been a timely life-saver for Kieran, enabling him to find his passion and purpose.

The studio was later delivered to others within the group. Over three days of studio loan, each person received six hours of studio time with a music leader, with similar great results and a number of unexpected outcomes. The young people had to set up the studio themselves (with phone support when needed), and this greatly improved their understanding of each piece of equipment and how it works.

During the following five months the team bought a further five mobile recording studios, and Kieran was trained to help set up his peers with the equipment. He's now a proud member of the Music Fusion team. In fact, many of the team members were former young people who used the studio's services.

What the young people get from their time at the studio isn't just an outlet for their musical talents – it's connection, quality friendships, communication skills, confidence, self-esteem and guidance, support and also challenge from the charity's leaders. They're treated with respect and spoken to as adults – something they're not always used to – and they respond in kind. Many are able to get their lives on track, and make something of themselves.

They're treated with respect and spoken to as adults – something they're not always used to – and they respond in kind.

Jinx takes no credit for these achievements, instead citing his team as the real superheroes. He's largely content with overseeing the business side of things these days, and knowing that the work everyone's doing is making a significant difference to the young people of the estate where he grew up as a boy.

In early September the charity released 'The Lockdown Sessions' – an E.P. of amazingly high-quality music, written, recorded and produced during lockdown. You can listen at: www.strongchoicemusic.bandcamp.com/album/lockdown-sessions.

Anyone wishing to make a donation to support the excellent work that Music Fusion do can contact info@musicfusion.org.uk.
Tel. 023 9249 2373.

13 YouTrust – Cath Parker

Cath Parker is the 'Cycling Without Age' co-ordinator at the YOU Trust – a Portsmouth based charity that supports vulnerable people across Hampshire, Dorset, Somerset, the Isle of Wight, and West Sussex.

'Cycling Without Age' is a non-profit global initiative which was founded in Copenhagen in 2012. As part of the initiative, volunteers take older people and care home residents out on electrically assisted 'trishaw' cycles, of which the YOU Trust now owns three. As part of the initiative, volunteers take older people and care home residents out on electrically assisted 'trishaw' cycles, of which the YOU Trust now owns three.

The rides are comfortable, joyful, free of charge, and enable passengers to experience the city and nature close-up, feeling the wind in their hair.

When the lockdown came into force, the cycles were put into temporary storage. People over the age of 70 were advised to self-isolate, and care homes were locked down completely, hence the service had to be temporarily paused. Not that business at the YOU Trust paused – they were busier than ever in some respects.

The Trust was part of the city's initial frontline Covid response team, delivering food parcels and medications to people in the community. Staff members were also helping people with enquiries relating to benefit entitlements, although this was done via telephone consultations.

For Cath, who does much of the organisation's admin work, it was an extremely busy time. She was manning the phone and responding to answerphones messages, dealing with emails, and taking referrals. As the only person working from the office building, she missed the buzz of having her colleagues around her. When the solitude began to affect her well-being, she switched to working mostly from home, going into the office only when she had to. It was a taste of what it might feel like not to see anyone all day – a reality for some of the trust's 'Cycling Without Age' passengers. Cath could really appreciate first-hand how an outing on the bikes would act as a wonderful pick-me-up for those who use the service.

August saw the delivery of a brand-new bike, as well as the careful reinstatement of rides. Mother and daughter Gladys Grimstead and Gill Stallard were the first to enjoy a ride since the early days of spring. Gladys, who's 103, had spent much of the lockdown period in her home watching TV, so it felt wonderful, once restrictions began to ease, to be out and about again. In contrast, Gill had been very busy throughout lockdown looking after her ten-year-old great grandson, keeping him busy with school work and fun activities, as well as shopping for, and visiting, her mum.

It was a taste of what it might feel like not to see anyone all day – a reality for some of the trust's 'Cycling Without Age' passengers.

The pair had a fabulous time on the bike, and thoroughly enjoyed smiling and waving to everyone as they passed by! Co-ordinator Cath loves the social side of her role, and is looking forward to the time when the team can all come back together in the office once more.

To join the ride, contact: 023 9206 5504.
cyclingwithoutage@theyoutrust.org.uk

14 Dementia Support - Dianne Gill

It's estimated that one in three people born in recent times will develop some form of dementia in their lifetime, so the chances are that the condition will touch all of us in some way in the years to come – indirectly if not personally. Dianne Gill is Corporate Partnerships Manager at Dementia Support – a charity based in Tangmere, near Chichester, that supports people and their families through the dementia journey before, during and after diagnosis

DEMENTIA SUPPORT

Sage House is the charity's community centre – a bright, colourful and modern building where people can access support, information, advice, day care, a large range of activities, therapies, a hairdressing salon, a smart zone, and a thriving community café.

It's the only centre in the whole of the UK which provides a 'one stop shop' for all things relating to dementia, including a diagnosis service, 'Dementia Friends' training for businesses and organisations, and even legal advice. It's also a happy and joyful place where the staff and volunteers love to have fun and make people laugh.

Sadly, they had to stop their day services in March when the country went into lockdown. They were, however, able to keep in contact with customers and their carers via telephone and *Zoom* chats. They created a well-being and activity pack to keep people stimulated throughout isolation, reaching out to parish town clerks, and via social media, to reach the elderly and isolated. To date, 4,500 packs have been sent out to people locally, nationally and internationally, with 77 new customers having signed up with the service at the time of writing.

About a month after the start of lockdown, Dianne and the team decided they were fed up with dressing down for work, and came up with the idea of 'Dress-up Friday', or D4D – *Dress-up 4 Dementia*. It started with them wearing smart workwear, then progressed to evening wear, then fancy dress of all kinds, from superheroes to circus acts! Local singer and entertainer Dawn Gracie is a supporter of the charity, and presented weekly, live 'Singalong Friday' shows via their *Facebook* page, culminating in a finale broadcast from Augusta Court's car park on 31st July. *Dress-up Fridays* continue as a monthly feature.

Not only did these events raise money for the charity, the photos on social media helped hugely to spread awareness of what they do, with over 50,000 views on *LinkedIn* alone. This helped to keep the team going, and gave enjoyment to their customers, friends and contacts. Many people would message them weekly to ask what the theme for the week was, and to encourage them not to stop!

The charity receives no government funding, and relies solely on donations and fundraising. They hope to continue the work they do for many years to come, and would love to build more centres and help other groups to do what they've done. Looking ahead, they can't wait to be fully operational again. Dianne and the team have missed the buzz and bustle of a busy centre, and are looking forward to the time when they can welcome everyone back once more.

For more information, or to help, please call: 01243 888 691, or email: info@dementia-support.org.uk

Dianne and the team have missed the buzz and bustle of a busy centre, and are looking forward to the time when they can welcome everyone back once more.

15

The Elizabeth Foundation for Deaf Children

The Elizabeth Foundation in Cosham has been providing *Ofsted* rated 'Outstanding' education and support services to pre-school deaf children and their families since 1981, helping every child to meet their full potential.

The centre's on-site nursery activities were suspended in March, following government guidelines for educational establishments. However, staff were determined to respond rapidly and effectively to support the children in digital, home-based learning.

Staff members quickly published lesson materials, activity sheets and hints and tips for parents of the centre's 80+ regular attendees. They recorded engaging videos including the children's favourite songs and stories, so they could practise their communication and see their teachers online.

Lockdown was an unsettling time for both the children and their parents - many of whom, in addition to worries about the virus, had concerns around delayed development, managing hearing technologies and postponed surgeries.

Staff continued to update care plans and monitor the progress of each child to ensure a continuity in support and development. They also made their online 'Let's Listen and Talk' programme freely available to any families of deaf children, increasing their resource to support the additional 400+ subscribers that signed up.

They were able to keep their hearing care centre going throughout the lockdown period, with the local *NHS Audiology* team and community midwives making use of their facilities to provide continuous care for local residents.

Deputy CEO, Karen Vaughan (BEM) said:
"It is so important for deaf children to have access to expert support to develop strong communication skills, which underpin opportunities to learn, to stay safe and maintain good mental health. At this particularly challenging time, it has been equally important for parents to be able to share their worries and concerns with our dedicated team."
Wonderful work, team!

To find out more, please go to: www.elizabeth-foundation.org, or call 02392 37 27 35

16 The Kings Theatre

When the country went into lockdown in late March 2020, it put the future of many theatres and centres for The Arts into jeopardy, with all events and income disappearing overnight.

THE KINGS THEATRE

The Kings Theatre in Southsea, a beautiful, Grade II* listed building designed by architect Frank Matcham, first opened for business in September 1907. The theatre has been through some rocky times in the years since then (at one point it was two weeks away from being bought by a well-known pub chain!), but thanks to the support and love of local people and visitors, it has survived throughout as a cultural hub of national importance, providing entertainment, outreach and educational work for the community.

The theatre experienced a short closure during *World War II*, and closed its doors again in late March 2020, following the government guidance.

May 2020 saw the 100th anniversary of the death of Frank Matcham – a chance to celebrate the genius of the man who'd designed this magnificent building along with a number of others, including the world-famous *London Coliseum* and *Palladium*. One glance up at the Kings' ceiling, or out across the auditorium, provides a flavour of his architectural talent, and is enough to fill almost anyone with awe. Events planned to mark the occasion at his venues across the country sadly had to be cancelled.

> *Whilst they awaited news of what the funding package would mean for them, they continued to innovate and adapt to secure their future.*

An impassioned letter from Kings' CEO Paul Woolf in June to Culture Secretary Oliver Dowden calling for a plan and guidance to safely re-open the theatre industry, was followed in July by a government announcement regarding a support package for The Arts. Whilst they awaited news of what the funding package would mean for them, they continued to innovate and adapt to secure their future.

The team took the closure as an opportunity to address the poor state of the carpet in the stalls – something that had been a common theme from customers for years. Because the theatre usually runs events and activities 350+ days a year, they'd never found a good time to do this. No-one could have imagined the difference it would make to the view when looking out over the theatre from the stage, or looking down from the Circles and Gallery. It has uplifted and transformed the entire look of the venue.

The theatre re-opened for business in September with strict safety protocols and a limited programme in place taking them up to the 'The Pompey Panto' Dick Whittington (re-imagined for the Covid era). In October they were awarded a significant chunk of funding from the *Government's Culture Recovery Fund*. As a registered charity with no Arts Council funding, this was a huge relief, and will help to make up for what they've lost this year.

The Kings Theatre is heavily reliant on the support and goodwill of its audiences and local community. Anyone wishing to help or find out more can visit the website: www.kingsportsmouth.co.uk

17 The Pompey Pals Charity & Museum

The Pompey Pals Charity was originally set up with the aim of commemorating the men who served in the *14th and 15th Battalions Hampshire Regiment, 1st and 2nd Portsmouth*, the Pompey Pals.

In 2014, Bob Beech, Chris Pennycook and Kevin Harfield worked with *Portsmouth Football Club* to produce a physical memorial to the Portsmouth battalions, which can be found by the main entrance to *Fratton Park*.

As a result of the community interest generated by the unveiling of the memorial, they made the decision to set up an independent charity to focus on the forthcoming centenary events of the *First World War*. Bob left the charity to focus on other projects in 2015, and Gareth Lewis was invited to join as chairman in 2017.

Portsmouth is rightly associated with having a rich Naval history, but a hundred years ago it was also an Army garrison town. Many people who live in the area today have family links to the military, so when the team opened the Pompey Pals Museum and Research Centre at *Ford Widley* in Cosham in 2018, they made the decision to focus on the personal stories and history of service from WWI to the present day. The charity's three main areas of activity are remembrance, education, and support for veterans.

The museum is full of fascinating equipment and memorabilia, and visitors are often wowed as they come through the doors. Far from being full of guns and weapons, the museum is full of personal items and stories that bring history to life.

2020 was going to be another big year of growth for The Pompey Pals, and the team had stepped up their events calendar, with lots of things planned throughout the year to commemorate dates of relevance to the city.

Their event on 10 January at *Kingston Cemetery*, commemorating the *Portsmouth Blitz*, went ahead as planned, but sadly, it was the only event to do so. Beyond that, when the country went into lockdown, all other planned activities had to be cancelled, cutting off the charity's main source of fundraising.

Unfortunately, they were unable to claim any government financial support to help them through. In previous years, their finances had fallen below the threshold where audited accounts were required, and they subsequently didn't qualify for any help. Additionally, they were unable to secure a rent payment holiday from their landlord, and very quickly, the charity's financial reserves were gone.

The friends were having to put their own money into keeping the premises going. Things got so bad that they were even having conversations with the charity's trustees and team of volunteers about potentially having to wrap the charity up, as they believed that they were finished. After all the years of hard work that everyone had put in, and the pride they felt for everything that they'd achieved, they were going to have to let it all go. It was so frustrating.

They'd applied, and been turned down, for several grants, before finally, at the 11th hour, managing to secure some funding from *Portsmouth City Council* that, alongside personal donations and online fundraising, would see them through until 2021. They'd been pulled back from the brink, and were thrilled to discover the support that was there for them in their time of need. It was a difficult year, but with help, they pulled through.

Looking ahead to 2021, chairman Gareth Lewis and co-founder Chris Pennycook are making plans in the hope that public events will be able to proceed, whilst ensuring that these plans are flexible, in case that's not possible. The key dates and events include the following:

10 January will be the 80th anniversary of the *Blitz* bombing raid on the city, which happened in 1941.

22nd May will be the 80th anniversary of the sinking of *HMS Hood*, sunk by the German battleship *Bismarck*, with the loss of over 1400 lives. Covid allowing, the team are planning a commemorative event in partnership with the city council's *Events Team*, and *Ubique Right of the Line Living History Group*, to be held on Southsea Common. This will include a remembrance service in the morning, and 1940s-style entertainment in the afternoon.

Every September for the last 5 years, the team have organised a special commemorative event in honour of all Portsmouth military personnel, past and present, over the last 150 years. The event planned for 11th and 12th September will be bigger and better than ever before, spanning two days rather than the customary one, and taking place in the city's *Guildhall Square*.

All being well, some fabulous events to look forward to, thanks to all at The Pompey Pals Charity (and those who support them) for ensuring that the area's rich military history is kept alive.

Lockdown gave us all a small taste of what it feels like to have our freedoms curtailed, and for a short while at least, to have certain items in short supply. May we never forget the sacrifices that were made for our freedom and liberty, and may we always remember how lucky we are.

To find out more about The Pompey Pals Charity please visit:
Web: www.pompeypals.org.uk
Facebook: www.facebook.com/PompeyPalsProject
Instagram: pompey_pals_charity
Twitter: @PompeyPals.

72 Years of the NHS – Sunday 5th July

5th July 2020 marked the 72nd birthday of the *National Health Service* (NHS) and social care system. 2020 was reported to be the most challenging year in NHS history, hence a final 'Clap for our Carers' was called to recognise and thank all NHS staff for their work and sacrifice in tackling the first wave of the virus.

NHS & KEY WORKER STORIES

When the country went into lockdown, many workers fell into one of three camps: those whose work stopped overnight and who had time on their hands; those who worked from home; and certain 'key workers' who had never been busier.

Key workers included NHS and healthcare staff, including administrative and cleaning personnel; those working in social care, education and childcare; the food (and essential items) chain; key public services; national and local government; utilities; public safety and national security; and transport workers. Children everywhere were delighted to hear the announcement from New Zealand's Prime Minister *Jacinda Ardern* that the Easter Bunny and Tooth Fairy were also considered essential workers.

Over 750,000 people signed up to the 'Your NHS Needs You' call for volunteers, engaging in activities from transporting patients to and from appointments, to collecting medicines, and telephone befriending.

On 26th March, the 'Clap for our Carers' movement was started in the UK by Dutch expatriate *Annemarie Plas*, who'd noticed a similar thing happening in the Netherlands. Every Thursday evening at 8pm for around nine weeks, people were encouraged to come out of their homes and clap (or bang pots and pans), for the NHS and care workers. From April, the appreciation was extended to all key workers, and the practice finally came to an end on Thursday 28th May as restrictions began to ease, and at Annemarie's request. Much of the country joined in with the clapping, including celebrities such as the *Beckhams*, politicians, and members of the royal family. There was one final public clap on Sunday 5th July at 5pm, to celebrate the NHS's 72nd birthday.

Schools and nurseries closed their doors to all except key workers' children, with various forms of home-schooling taking place for everyone else. Research by the *Office for National Statistics* indicates that an average of 11 hours' home study was completed per child per week, with many completing no academic work at all. Colleges and universities closed at around the same time, taking their learning online too. Having to home-school their children (as well as work from home, in many cases) gave many parents a greater appreciation for the job that teachers do, and even helped children to appreciate school life more.

We are privileged in the UK that every child has the right to an education, and our children learn at least as much informally, from interacting with others, as they do from the formal learning curriculum. Teachers are heroes, and help to shape the character and values of our children. We should probably value and reward them more than we currently do.

Here are some stories from the front-line.

18 Pip Wilson

Pip Wilson is an accident and emergency (A&E) doctor who works at University Hospital Southampton. She, her husband Dan (also a doctor) and their little boy Will moved to the Southampton area in 2018 for work.

Pip was around 14 weeks pregnant in March 2020 when a routine scan revealed some foetal anomalies. She saw a specialist the very next day, who confirmed that the baby had a syndrome that would very likely prove to be life threatening, and so Pip and Dan were faced with the heart-breaking situation of terminating the pregnancy.

This was just before the country went into lockdown, and the following day was to be Pip's best friend (who is also her little boy Will's godmother)'s wedding, which they felt they couldn't miss. The procedure was subsequently scheduled for after the wedding, and Pip, looking obviously pregnant at this stage but not wanting to put any dampeners on the day, had to go along with everyone's happy congratulations, and hands on her bump.

Soon afterward, she was back in hospital having the procedure. Everything went as smoothly as it could have done, and the staff were amazing – even sorting out a funeral service for the baby. It was 6 weeks before they could get a timeslot as the service was so stretched (it was the height of the pandemic), and it felt like a strange little ceremony with only Pip, Dan and Will in attendance, and no flowers allowed.

Pip took two weeks off work to recover, but found it tough being on her own at home with a toddler, grieving the loss of her baby, and with no face-to-face support. She was thankful to get back to work after this time, despite it being the most unnerving time of her career, as she'd felt guilty taking time out, and needed to detach from her difficult thoughts and feelings.

Helping other people again gave Pip a different focus, and enabled her to work through her grief. Things were far from normal back at work, with everything arranged differently, new protocols, and a different category of patients from A&E's usual regulars and the "worried well". Pip was placed into Resus, where 90% of patients were struggling with Covid-19, and starving of oxygen. She got to the end of many her shifts feeling physically and mentally broken, albeit thankful for the distraction of work, and for having a semblance of structure and busy-ness back in her life.

Pip and Dan had established a new routine of getting changed out of their work scrubs immediately on arriving back home after a shift, and putting them straight in the washing machine on a 90° wash cycle. They'd never done so much washing as during this time, and on the May bank holiday Sunday, their washing machine broke down with a half-washed load inside.

Pip rang her local white goods store, *Hedge End Domestics*, and left a message on their answer-phone, expecting to get a call back on the Tuesday. She was amazed to get a call just 10 minutes later from the store's co-owner Susan Butt, who not only agreed to send an engineer to look at the machine, but also offered to collect the half-washed scrubs and launder them herself, which she later did.

Susan's husband, Ken, went out to look at the machine the very next day (Bank Holiday Monday) and managed to fix it, refusing to take any payment. Pip was so thankful to the pair for their kindness, and the first-class customer service they provided to a family that they didn't even know.

In fact, lockdown seemed to inspire all manner of acts of kindness, with a colleague of Pip's reporting having his petrol paid for by someone he didn't know at 3am one morning. It seemed as though kindness went viral too, during the Covid-19 pandemic!

There comes a time in life when, after years of our parents worrying about us, the tables turn, and we begin to worry more about them. Pip and Dan's parents aren't local, and they were sadly unable to see them for months during the lockdown. Pip's dad, who has chronic obstructive pulmonary disease (COPD) continued working through the lockdown but developed a chest infection, thankfully recovering with medicines. Pip's mum was so concerned about her own mother at this time, who normally relied on different carers visiting every day, that she cancelled the usual carers and moved in with her temporarily, to shield her from the risk of infection.

Lockdown seemed to put people more in touch with a sense of their own and their loved ones' mortality – that life isn't guaranteed for any of us, and is a blessing we should never take for granted. It seemed to make us more appreciative of our lives, of the people in them, and even of our world, which seemed to be flourishing with less in the way of human activity and pollution. It also gave us a bit more reflection time, and brought home a sense of what's really important, making us question our former priorities.

In life before Covid, Pip had been on a busy merry-go-round of work mixed with a timetable of activities with Will, and very little in between. During lockdown life became less noisy and structured and more spontaneous, with the family getting to know their neighbours better, and having more fun times and playful family interactions. They also found themselves better off financially, being unable to spend money in cafes, on shopping as a pastime, and so on.

Pip slowed down a bit and learned how to relax, discovering a love and a talent for gardening. She painted her shed. She played in the paddling pool with her son, and enjoyed being in the moment with him, watching his rapid development. She came to the conclusion that she doesn't have to fill every moment with an activity, and that it's ok to say "No" sometimes, and be a bit more selective about what she gives her time to.

What a fabulous outcome, Pip. Many thanks to you, your husband and all of your colleagues for putting your lives lives on the line in dedicated service to the NHS and to the community. We wish you and your family all the very best in the times to come.

Just before going to print, Pip advised that she is currently 23 weeks pregnant – the best news we've had all year!

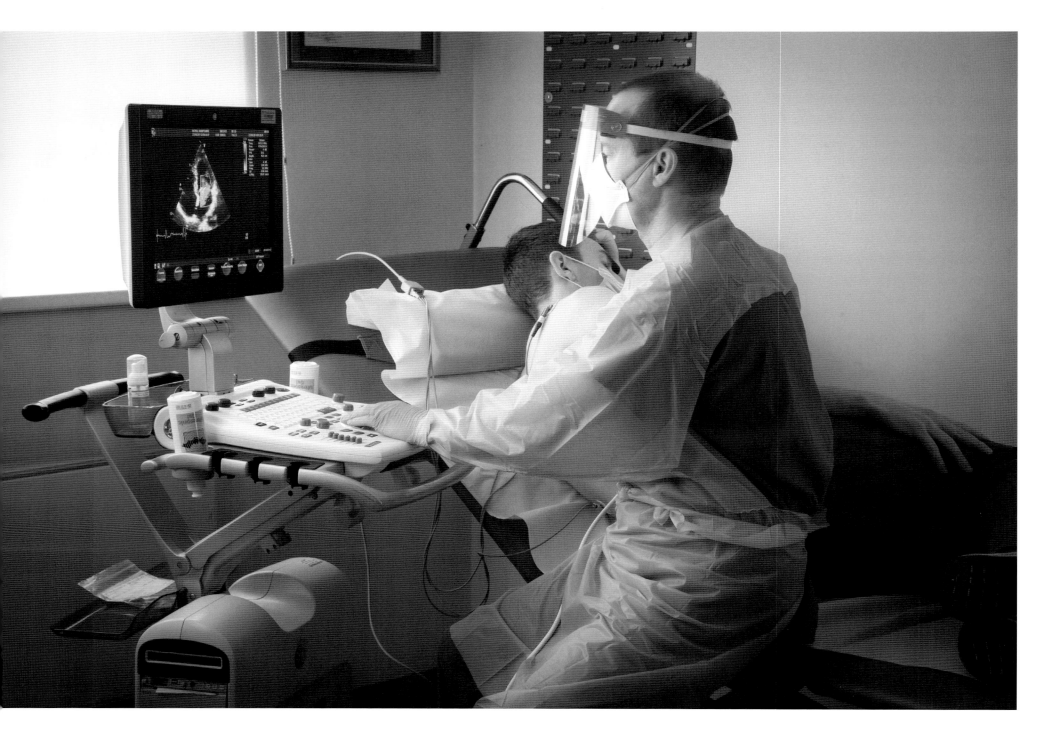

Ian Treveil

Ian Treveil is a retired Army major and clinical physiologist. After serving 30 years in the *Royal Army Medical Corps*, his transition into civilian life (and a second career as a locum), was relatively smooth.

Ian spent five years at *Frimley Park Hospital* near Camberley before starting a new contract in Cardiology at the *Royal Hampshire County Hospital* in Winchester in October 2019.

In preparation for the lockdown, the hospital underwent many changes. Senior leaders had a relatively good idea of what was coming, based on the patterns which had emerged within other countries, and so the hospital was adapted for upcoming needs. Certain wards were allocated for assessing and caring for Covid patients, and normal day patient clinics were cancelled. Ian's department was moved into Outpatients, and he was able (as a member of the *Bishops Waltham Rotary Club*) to donate some televisions to the hospital's newly created isolation rooms.

Within a few weeks, the department became incredibly busy, with many working extra hours. The work involved a lot of echocardiogram scans (not dissimilar to pregnancy ultrasound scans), as well as report writing, risk assessments and patient prioritising. Scanning patients requires an 'up close and personal' hands-on approach, and many of the patients Ian saw during this time were Covid positive. The nature of the virus wasn't fully understood at this stage, and safety was therefore unknown, and a significant concern.

On top of his hospital scrubs, Ian had to wear a theatre-style gown, and be double-gloved, with his head covered and face masked. Everything had to be changed between patients, which took time and meant they weren't able to get through as many scans as usual. With the amazing Springtime weather we were having, it was very hot, very sticky and very energy draining; however, Ian had had 'training' for this in the trenches in Iraq wearing chemical warfare coveralls and respirator in 40°+ temperatures. If he could survive that, he knew he could survive this too!

There were a lot of gifts and freebies being donated by the local community for the staff, and this made a huge difference to how everyone felt.

Well-being was important, and staff were encouraged to take regular fresh-air breaks. Morale was pretty good, in general. There were a lot of gifts and freebies being donated by the local community for the staff, and this made a huge difference to how everyone felt. One employee's husband who normally runs a school tuckshop, donated a load of stock that would have gone out of date before September, and they were also given lots of Easter eggs. Local Women's Institute branches donated cakes and baked goods throughout, and care was taken to distribute these evenly between the wards.

The staff worked together and looked out for one another. Some struggled emotionally more than others, and were supported by their colleagues. It was particularly difficult for some of the younger, live-in staff staying in single accommodation within the hospital grounds, being unable to go out (except for a daily walk), or see family and friends.

Despite the difficulties, Ian felt fortunate to have the normality of a daily routine and a purpose. He was grateful for walks after work with his wife where he had the opportunity to talk and download the day, and he found that people in the community were more likely to strike up conversation during this time, and look out for one another. The Postmaster at Waltham Chase Post-Office worked particularly hard to support the community, and the village's Facebook page was a hub for requests and willing volunteers.

Ian's workload eventually slowed down following the initial spike in the early days, and then started to pick up again as some nasty cardiac-related side effects from the virus began to appear. Research was ongoing throughout, with guidance coming through regularly, and the teams learned and adapted as they went. Normal outpatient clinics were reintroduced in July, and they began to catch up on the backlog of people whose treatment or investigation had been delayed due to the lockdown.

Ian is looking forward to some semblance of normality and social events returning sometime soon. He's also looking forward to a walking holiday in the UK in the early Autumn, and to bringing the whole family together again for his daughter's wedding next year (rescheduled from September 2020 to May 2021).

Thank you, Ian, not just for 30+ years' service to Queen and country, but also for your selfless service to the NHS, and continuing to care for patients during this challenging and uncertain time when your own safety wasn't certain.

We salute you!

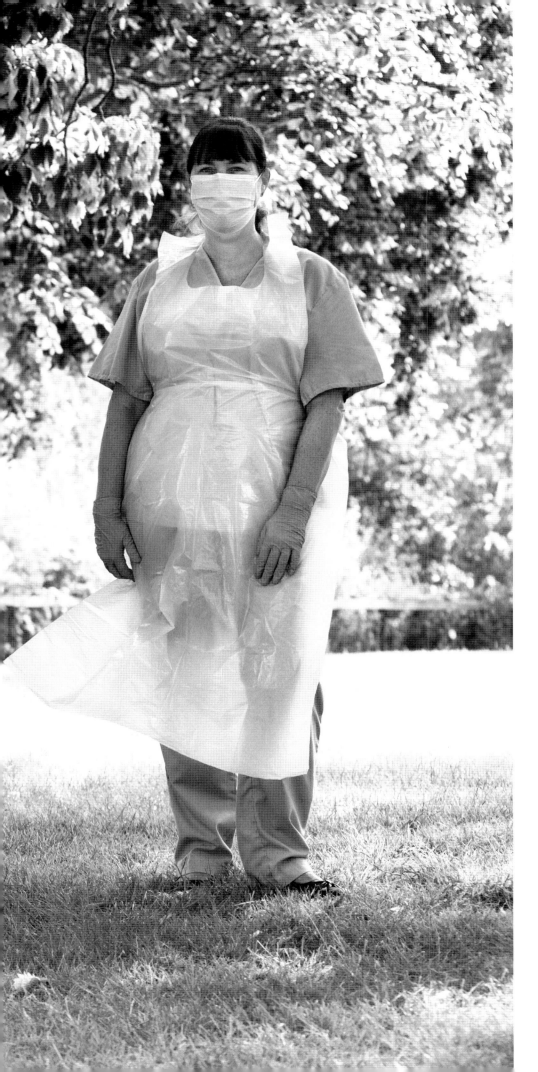

20

Tracy & Vic Martin

In September 2019, administrator Tracey Martin and her taxi-driver husband Vic gave up their jobs to go back-packing around the world – intending to return home at the end of May 2020.

Their travels took them to Asia, Bali, Australia, and they were in New Zealand in March when they realised that the situation with Covid-19 had become sufficiently serious that they needed to return home.

The day after arriving back home, the country went into lockdown, and their lives changed dramatically overnight. Having not seen their family or friends for six months, they were still unable to do so. It was especially upsetting for their four young grandchildren, who couldn't understand why they couldn't see Nana and Pops, now that they'd returned home.

The couple found work at Alton Community Hospital – Vic as a cleaner and Tracey as a kitchen assistant. They worked three or four days a week, getting up at 5:15 am each day to help clean the hospital and serve the patients – some of whom were Covid positive. Vic also had to assist with moving bodies to the mortuary.

Prior to the lockdown, they had been set to arrive home on 29th May, in time for a family weekend away in Dorset, and a couple of weeks afterwards, a huge joint party to celebrate Vic's 60th and one of their daughter's 30th birthdays. Of course, all events had to be cancelled.

What should have been the trip of a lifetime may not have ended the way they'd have liked, but they were thankful they made the decision to return home when they did, so their family didn't need to worry about them.

In September, Tracey started a new job within the NHS as a team administrator. She is already dreaming of future adventures, and hopes that one day in the not-too-distant future, she and Vic will be able to pick up their travels where they left off.

We hope so too. Bon voyage to you both!

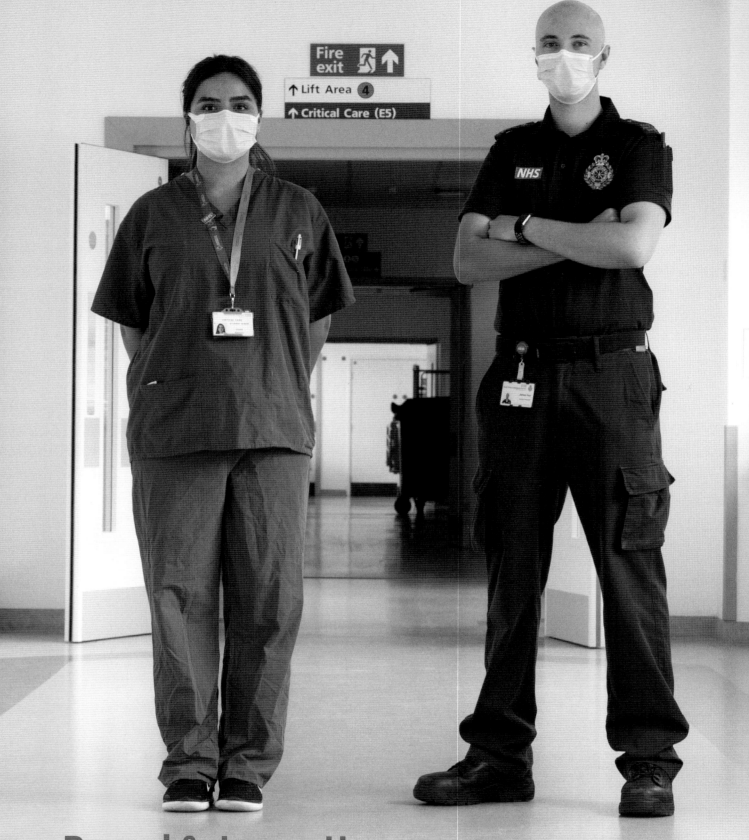

21 Diana Rasoul & James Hey

During the pandemic, a number of nursing and paramedic students from the *University of Portsmouth* volunteered their services on the NHS frontline. Amongst them were Diana Rasoul and James Hey.

Diana Rasoul

2020 was a very strange year for 23-year-old third year nursing student Diana Rasoul. The academic years of her nursing degree ran from February through to December. She'd done a month of academic study in February, and was a few weeks into her second and final work placement on the Orthopaedic ward at the *Queen Alexandra Hospital*, Cosham, when she received a letter from the University advising all students to finish their placements with immediate effect, due to the virus.

There were no lectures in the time that followed, but the students attended weekly *Zoom* updates with their lecturers and tutors. They were advised that the *Nursing and Midwifery Council* (NMC) was looking for undergraduate students, and nurses who'd left the nursing register, to come forward and supplement the workforce. Diana's partner and brothers are both doctors, and had been working throughout. Whilst it was an uncertain and frightening time, and there was a lot of anxiety amongst the students, Diana didn't want to just sit at home. She volunteered, and was fortunate enough to be accepted onto her first-choice ward, the Intensive Care Unit (ICU) at the *Queen Alexandra*.

It was a strange world in those early days, and everyone seemed to be running on adrenaline. Diana felt lost and confused at times, and then at the end of her first week she received news that her father, who lives in London, had been taken into hospital with the virus. The family had reported him feeling unwell, tired and achy for a while, and when this developed into extreme shortness of breath, they called an ambulance.

It was a worrying and anxious time, and Diana found it hard being away from her family and not knowing when she'd see them next. She was working nights, and would sometimes cry before going on duty. She felt scared, hot (in all the protection equipment) and bothered, and at times questioned why she'd willingly volunteered to take on the work. Her brother and her partner were her inspiration to keep going, and her nursing colleagues were very supportive. As difficult as it was, Diana felt honoured to be playing her part in supporting the NHS and its patients through the crisis.

Diana's father made a full recovery, having been in Intensive Care and intubated for a couple of weeks. He later returned to work, grateful that things had turned out well for him. Diana did return home to London for a visit when it was safe to do so, observing social distancing in the garden. When cases of the virus began to climb again, she decided to stay away again, so as not to put anyone at risk.

Towards the end of Diana's four months on the ICU, all the Covid patients had gone. She stayed on for a while afterwards before taking a bit of time off and leaving to begin completing the paperwork for her degree.

At the time of printing (November), Diana was completing a final assignment and putting together her dissertation. She's due to qualify in early December, and has already received a job offer, which she hopes to takes up after Christmas.

Diana is excited to get stuck in to her career as a fully-fledged nurse. Her aim is to become a Critical Care Practitioner in the next few years, as she's been so inspired by those in the role at the *Queen Alexandra*.

James Hey

22-year-old first year paramedic student James Hey, from Gosport, volunteered for a patient transport role during lockdown, taking people with essential appointments and procedures to and from hospital.

After initial training in April, he worked from a base in Gosport, where his colleagues were helpful and welcoming, treating him as one of their own right away. As part of a two-person team, he wasn't permitted to drive, but gained a lot of experience in manual handling and many other tasks.

James had wanted to be a television presenter as a schoolboy, but in 2012 when his grandfather, Don, fell ill, he was inspired to change track by two paramedics at Frimley Park Hospital. Their swift actions when Don collapsed had given him a bit more time, meaning that James and his mum (who'd had to fly back to the UK on the second day of their holiday in Lanzarote) were able to see him and say goodbye before he passed away. He was in an induced coma when they arrived, and eventually the sad decision was made to turn off the machines.

James was consoled by the fact that hearing is believed to be the last sense to go in the process of dying, even when a patient is unconscious. All immediate family members were at Don's bedside in his final moments, and James hopes to be able to do for other families one day what those two observant and responsive paramedics had done for his own family.

Outside of his patient transport duties, James was a frequent visitor to his grandmother during lockdown, who's physically fit but has advanced dementia. He would call her most days to check she was ok, and also did her shopping during this time.

James enjoyed his experience of working in the patient transport service, and it confirmed that the role of paramedic was a good career choice for him. Working with all the different people he met gave him greater insight into the role, and the contact he had with patients enabled him to build his skills and confidence. It's also given him a few new stories to tell, such as the time he was bitten by a patient's Rottweiler whilst on duty, and ended up in Accident & Emergency himself!

Camping has been a big tradition in James' family, from his grandparents, to his parents, and now to James and his partner. Despite the virus, they managed to get a week away in a little log cabin near St Austell in Cornwall, with a firepit for cooking and hot water. They also enjoyed a spot of wild camping in the New Forest.

James hopes to be able to do for other families one day what those two observant and responsive paramedics had done for his own family.

James loves the outdoor lifestyle, and believes that fresh air is good for the immune system. Many of us are shallow breathers, meaning that we don't always cleanse our lungs of the bacteria that can lurk in the base regions. The deep breathing of fresh, clean air can do a lot to help treat respiratory conditions and infections, including Covid-19. James believes that the body is self-healing in the right conditions, and that with a bit of self-care and good nutrition, most otherwise healthy people will be "as right as rain" again a few weeks after catching the virus.

Inspired by his partner Ellisha (a prolific reader), James has enjoyed escaping into the world of fantasy books in his off-duty time this year, which has proven to be a great antidote to reality! He highly recommends that anyone stuck at home should pick up a good book and escape for a while into another world, too.

Now in the second year of his degree course, James and his fellow students are being encouraged to think of topics for their dissertations. James is considering exploring the impact of mental health on diabetes, which can be profound, although it's often overlooked.

We have no doubt that both James and Diana have very bright futures ahead of them in their chosen fields, and wish them both every success.

22 Charles Tick

When the country went into lockdown, 32-year-old Charles Tick was in the third and final year of his nursing degree, studying at the University of Portsmouth.

Charles had loved dressing up as a doctor when he was a little boy, and when his mum developed cancer a few years later, he was struck by how kind the nurses were. He decided that he wanted to be a nurse when he grew up instead, but ended up doing a number of different roles before waking up one day and making the decision to fulfil his childhood ambition.

He'd saved enough money from the well-paid sales job he'd been doing to fund further studies, so he started by taking evening classes to re-do some of the GCSEs that he hadn't done as well in as he'd have liked at school. After that he took an online access course, before signing up to do his nursing degree in 2017. It was quite a journey, but he believed in himself and never lost sight of his goal.

When the lockdown was announced in March, Charles continued with his assignments and dissertation. He also stepped forward to supplement the NHS workforce following the NMC's request for volunteers, and worked full-time at *Queen Alexandra Hospital*, Cosham, in the Haematology and Oncology department, mostly providing cancer care. He loved it, but it wasn't easy – in fact it was quite daunting in the early days when no-one knew much about the virus, and it was often exhausting. Thankfully his nursing colleagues were really supportive, and thankful for the extra help.

Communication updates and meetings were held daily, and as resources became available, the hospital was stringent in their safety measures and testing. Counselling was available to any member of staff who wanted it, and Charles felt safe and supported.

During this time he particularly looked forward to his daily walk, and enjoyed the fact that people seemed more open to talking to one another than he'd previously noted. It was often the only social contact he had outside of work, except from when he was home with his partner and housemate. It was also hard being unable to visit his family in Kent. The family are close, and he missed his grandparents, twin brother and his brother's children.

Despite the difficulties, they were also many positives – not least of which was having his portrait painted by Kent-based artist Lydia Spearink, as part of *Tom Croft's #portraitsfornhsheroes* campaign.

During lockdown, award-winning Oxford-based portrait artist, Tom Croft, had posted a video on *Instagram* saying he would paint a free portrait of the first NHS key worker to contact him. He also suggested that other portrait artists might like to do the same, as part of a virtual exhibition.

Charles's partner secretly submitted a photo and nomination to Lydia, who painted an amazing portrait which his partner presented to him as a surprise one morning. He'd just got home following a particularly tiring night shift, and the beautiful painting and touching inscription provided an emotional moment that he'll always remember.

As to the future, Charles has decided to go on and study for a master's degree, once he's completed two full years of nursing practice. His long-term goal is to work for *Macmillan Cancer Support*, in palliative care.

He loved it, but it wasn't easy – in fact it was quite daunting in the early days when no-one knew much about the virus, and it was often exhausting.

Charles received the news that he'd passed his nursing degree in August. He believes that if you have a passion for something, you should just go and do it - not for the medals or for any kind of status (he still doesn't feel like a hero, and maintains he was just doing a job), but rather, for the love of it.

What a great message! Many congratulations Charles, and every good wish for your future.

23 Hilary Glanville

Hilary Glanville works as a higher-level teaching assistant at *Padnell Infant School* in Cowplain. During lockdown she worked for one day a week teaching the children of key workers – mostly playing outside, and with a maximum of nine children at a time.

When the Government decided that schools were to re-open, Hilary was concerned. The school was only able to open to Year R children due to limited resources, and she wondered how the school's four and five-year-old children would manage with so few toys to play with, sitting at tables for formal lessons, and not being with all of their friends.

Government guidelines recommended that classroom sizes be kept to a maximum of 15, with children kept within 'bubbles' (groups) of no more than four, and unable to mix with children in other bubbles. This was a massive challenge for all concerned, as it was so far removed from the usual way of schooling infants – through interactive play, and with very little formal teaching.

Toys and books had to be kept to a minimum, sanitised after each use, and then left for 24 hours. No soft furnishings or dressing-up clothes were allowed, and there were no 'home corners' (learning areas for role play, based on familiar surroundings and items in the home).

For the first two weeks, Hilary oversaw a classroom of just four children, along with a Learning Support Assistant – a formerly unheard-of ratio within state education! The children were amazing, and quickly adapted to the social distancing and frequent hand washing. Gradually, over the weeks, more children came back to school, and numbers climbed up to 12 towards the end, which included some Year 1 & 2 children too.

Whilst it was challenging having three different year groups in one class, somehow they managed. The younger children didn't seem to notice that they had more learning time, less play time and fewer toys and resources. With only one small box of bats and balls to use each playtime, over the weeks those items were magically transformed into ice creams, animals and many other things in the children's imaginations. It was fabulous to observe the creativity and imagination of the children as they played, and whilst the outdoor play equipment and gym were out of bounds, the children were too busy running their ice cream shop and organising football and tennis games to even notice, or to remember what it had been like to swing from the bars and fly down the slides.

The playground was split into small zones for each bubble, and space was very restricted. Of course, the children were limited to playing only with those within their bubbles, so there were many friends that didn't get to see or speak to one another, even though they were all in school together.

It was a strange time for the adults in school too, with many staff members avoiding each other in the corridors, and some working from home. A lot of time was spent washing down tables, chairs and toys, and teaching using online resources such as videos from *BBC Bitesize* and stories on *YouTube*.

Hilary found it very difficult when a child was crying (perhaps because they were missing their mum, or had scraped their knee), not being able to give them a hug. It was also hard remembering not to lean in when helping someone with their writing.

Hilary found it very difficult when a child was crying (perhaps because they were missing their mum, or had scraped their knee), not being able to give them a hug.

She had concerns about how they would maintain the protocols in September when the school re-opened to classrooms of 30 again, but distancing had been relaxed by that point, and it wasn't a problem. They'd survived the early challenges, and the children had proved to be amazingly resilient.

Well done to all at *Padnell Infant School*, and to schools and teachers everywhere. You've shown us how amazing you are, even in the hardest of circumstances. We feel sure that, whatever happens next, you'll find a way of making things work, and flourishing into the future.

BUSINESS STORIES

The spread of the virus disrupted not just lives, but also livelihoods, with many industries and businesses forced to close completely. Whilst the retail sector had been struggling for a number of years in the build-up to 2020, more famous retail brands went into administration during lockdown, including *M&Co*, *Monsoon*, *Cath Kidston*, *Laura Ashley*, *Victoria's Secret*, *Oasis*, *Warehouse*, *Bensons for Beds*, *Harveys*, *Oak Furnitureland*, and *GO Outdoors*.

Businesses that flourished included online shopping outlets, supermarkets, home improvement stores, delivery services, video-conferencing providers, funeral services and those selling health-related supplements. Aside from retail outlets, other businesses and industries that typically floundered included transport companies, the travel and tourism industry, sports and entertainment, investment banking, and oil and petrol companies.

Most business insurance policies didn't include cover for pandemic-related business interruption. The Government stepped in with a generous financial rescue package, although this excluded a reported three million of the country's five million self-employed people – approximately 10% of the workforce.

Many were forced to completely rethink their operating models in order to overcome the challenges they were facing, and maximise any opportunities that were present. In some cases, this meant a minor pivot – in others, a complete reinvention. People were forced to get very creative in their thinking in order to survive, and it was tough, with many small business owners going under, and others resorting to crowdfunding and food banks to survive.

Whilst in some cases business picked up when restrictions began to ease, many businesses continued to struggle. Predicted redundancy numbers in the UK (from employers planning 20 or more redundancies) shot up almost sevenfold in June and July of 2020, compared to the same time period in 2019, with unemployment figures predicted to hit the four million mark in 2021.

Even if the virus was to disappear as quickly as it had appeared, things had changed – habits had begun to change, and it seemed unlikely that we would go back to life and business exactly as they had been, pre-Covid. Some aspects of our former habits and ways of working weren't sustainable, and the planet had been suffering for it. Businesses realised that they didn't need such big offices and buildings in town and city centres; nor did every meeting or event need to be held face-to-face. Working from home, where it was possible and managed appropriately, worked pretty well for many. Some of us gained hours a day back in saved commuting time, enabling greater work/life balance. As tough as things had been for many businesses, there were definitely some benefits too.

Business is likely to get tougher and more competitive in the future, and those most likely to thrive will be the more sustainable, lower-carbon businesses that seek to do some good in the world, benefiting people and planet. As Sir Richard Branson once said, "Doing good is good for business".

24

Phoenix Project Solutions (Business Innovation South Expo) - Lara Bull

Lara Bull runs Phoenix Project Solutions, offering support for growing businesses across the south. She is also the creator of the *Business Innovation South Expo* for businesses in the science, technology, engineering and innovation sectors.

On the back of the success of the first expo held in 2019, Lara was gearing up for a bumper event in September 2020 with a large number of exhibitors having signed up, and then the lockdown was announced, and plans for events of all kinds were put on hold.

It would have been easy in the circumstances for Lara to feel frustrated and despondent that her plans were seemingly being thwarted, and there may have been a moment or so when that was the case. However, she quickly made her mind up that she would continue working towards September in the hope that the situation would allow it, whilst also planning a back-up date for the following April.

Uncertainty was the theme as the year unfolded, and with so many things outside of Lara's control, her plans had to be very flexible. The unknown can leave us feeling stressed and anxious, and Lara found an antidote to that in her garden.

The previous year, with all the time, energy and attention she'd put into launching her inaugural event, she'd had no time at all to invest in or enjoy her lovely garden. Fast-forward to 2020, and the lockdown gave her the opportunity to love her garden back to life again. She found the act of mindfully tending to the plants and shrubs and connecting with the soil very calming, and her garden responded by coming back more beautifully than ever.

Lara believes this 'green time' helped to sustain her mental well-being throughout the lockdown period, and enabled her to think things through calmly, and rework her plans. She believes that people can draw a lot of strength and peace from nature, as well as enjoying the beauty and bounty that's the reward for your efforts.

Another bonus from lockdown has been the quality time Lara's been able to spend with her teenaged children, who've enjoyed having their Mum at home more, and also with her own mum, who has sadly experienced a few health issues this year. They have drawn closer together as a family, and appreciated the opportunity to connect at an even deeper level.

There are always benefits to be found, even in the most difficult of times. Lara's determined to make the most of the opportunities that life presents her with, and her hard work, dedication and persistence will stand her in good stead.

Onward and upwards, Lara, and we wish you all the best for the *Business Innovation South Expo 2021*. It's going to be epic!

25 The Akash Restaurant

The Akash restaurant, established in Southsea in the 1970s by George Ahmed, and now run largely by George's sons Jafor (Jaf) and Forhad (Faz), is Portsmouth's longest serving Indian restaurant.

Older brother Jaf looks after the people-oriented 'front of house' side of the operation, whilst younger brother Faz focuses on the food-oriented 'back of house' aspect. Dad George is the wise head that reportedly pops in now and then to tell the boys they're doing it all wrong! Whilst the trio can differ in their ideas, they share great synergy, and generally reach a consensus when it comes to decision-making.

When the government began advising vulnerable people to stay home in March 2020, and restaurant closures were looking imminent, one of the first things the brothers did was donate 30 curries (plus accompaniments) to a team of nurses at *Queen Alexandra Hospital* in Cosham on *Mother's Day*. Faz had gone to school with one of the nurses there, and was aware that many of them would be unable to visit their mums and families that day, due to shielding and other restrictions. He hoped the food would bring a smile and help boost morale.

The family have always been community minded, but the brothers did everything they could during lockdown to help local people that they'd heard were in need, including taking milk, eggs, flour, bananas, toilet rolls, antibac handwash and other items, to those who needed them.

When the formal lockdown was announced, the brothers were faced with furloughing most of their staff, reducing the team down from 30 to just five. After an initial crisis meeting, they agreed to expand their takeaway service (formerly only about 10% of the business) to include new food delivery channels *Uber*, *Deliveroo* and *Just Eat*. Administrator Maria, a student from Portugal, got to work setting up all the contract agreements, and the delivery business was ready to go.

The following few weeks felt like a rollercoaster ride. Business was booming, and the phone was ringing constantly. The first day of going live with deliveries, Maria, who dealt with the delivery admin and took the order tickets through to the kitchen, thought the chefs were going to lock her out, due to the sheer volume of orders!

Maria, who dealt with all the delivery admin and took the order tickets through to the kitchen, thought the chefs were going to lock her out, due to the sheer volume of orders!

Every day brought new challenges and new government updates, announcements and directives. The family made adjustments as the situation evolved, and when each day came to an end, they would sit down together to discuss the latest updates, and plan their actions for the following day.

The early weeks of lockdown were tiring and stressful, with Jaf averaging between two and four and four hours' sleep a night. Conversely, he reports feeling really 'alive' during this time... running on adrenaline, and fuelled by his desire to face the challenge.

During service, their equipment struggled to keep up with the demand, and extra staff had to be brought in to help. On a couple of occasions, production was overwhelmed, and the food didn't meet their usual standard. The feedback afterwards was difficult to receive, and the brothers spent a lot of time discussing how they could improve, and prevent it from happening again.

Jaf was busy overseeing the operation much of the time, but loved being released to help with deliveries. This gave him the chance to breathe, and on the odd occasion, pop into his favourite bubble tea shop for a quick pit-stop! It also gave him an appreciation for how much customers valued the service, when he saw how happy and excited they became when the food arrived.

Throughout it all, the team were amazing. Everyone stepped up to the mark and went above and beyond the call of duty. Team member Rosie, who lives close to the restaurant, responded to a call for help by leaving her dinner half-eaten to dash back to work. Along with another team member, Yamin, Rosie looked after the business when Jaf and Faz's mum Monuara became ill with a liver problem, and the brothers were taking her back and forth to hospital.

The team drew very close during lockdown. They would gather together around a table to talk when they could, and the 'Front of House' and 'Back of House' teams got to know each other better, forming deeper friendships and even a burgeoning romance! It wasn't just business that was discussed during these times, but also well-being in terms of what was happening in everyone's lives – who needed what in the way of support, and so on. During *Ramadan* the whole team ate together too, as the sun was setting. It was a special time that they'll always remember fondly.

In early July, as restrictions began to relax, the restaurant re-opened with extra hygiene and social distancing measures in place to ensure safety. The brothers opted to take part in the government's 'Eat Out to Help Out' scheme, which they recall as the craziest time ever, with Covid-19 taking a holiday on Mondays, Tuesdays and Wednesdays to help boost the economy!

The Akash's customers remained loyal and supportive throughout, with some placing orders three or four times a week, and one customer even ordering daily. Food was one of the main things that people had to look forward to during lockdown, and it was wonderful for the family to realise just how much their business meant to people.

George and his sons have built up a lot of goodwill over the years. The Akash is a business with heart, and customers have said they'd do anything to ensure its survival. George, Jaf and Faz are all mindful of the fact that they wouldn't have a business if it wasn't for their amazing staff and customers – all of whom seem to really care about the business.

The quality of the food at The Akash has always been really important, but the quality of the welcome, hospitality and warmth that customers are shown is probably the thing that keeps them coming back.

Thank you, Team Akash, for working so hard to keep the community fed and happy throughout lockdown. Very best wishes to Mrs Ahmed.

26

Portsmouth Distillery - Vince Noyce, Giles Collighan & Dich Oatley

In 2018, former Royal Navy officers Vince Noyce, Giles Collighan, and drinks industry professional Dich Oatley set up The Portsmouth Distillery at Fort Cumberland, Southsea, making artisan gin, rum and cyder.

The team achieved considerable success early on, winning a number of local and international awards, before the lockdown halted operations in March.

As a relatively new company without much in the way of collateral, they were concerned for their business – not least because a significant part of their revenue had come from hosting tours of the premises – all of which had to be cancelled. However, when supplies of hand sanitiser around the country started to run out, the partners quickly spotted an opportunity, and diverted operations towards the production of alcohol-based hand sanitising products. This helped, in part, to make up for the lost tour revenue, leaving the trio in a relatively healthy financial position.

During this time, they were also able to finalise development on their latest product 'Tudor Gin', from which a substantial percentage of the profits will go to *The Mary Rose Trust*. They hope to hold a gala launch at *The Mary Rose Museum* once it's safe to do so.

Sales of gin have been on the increase for some time in the UK, and gin was reportedly the best-selling spirit online during the lockdown, with sales of flavoured varieties in particular going up 125% in March on the same period the previous year. Stockpiling is likely to be the main reason for the increase, although the invention of the gin-based 'Quarantini' cocktail probably helped to boost sales too!

The trio had set an aim at the start of the year to increase public awareness of their business, and in a strange way the Covid crisis helped them to achieve this. Daily deliveries in their branded van helped to get their name seen, and they've decided to maintain free delivery, for the time being, to those with PO- postcodes, as a way of thanking their local customers for keeping them going during the pandemic.

From October, they were able to reintroduce their tours for small groups. Previously they've also hired out their premises for parties and private events (supplying marquees where required), and are looking forward to the day when they can bring these events back.

Looking ahead to 2021, the friends plan to open their first retail outlet in the former *John Lewis/Knight & Lee* building on Palmerstone Road, Southsea, where they'll sell their own products and those of other producers.

Cheers Vince - Cheers Giles - Cheers Dich. Here's to new ventures!

Quattro Foods - Sam Brower

Sam Brower is the managing director of Quattro Foods in Portsmouth - a premium bespoke food manufacturer specialising in the development and manufacture of exclusive food products for the restaurant, retail, foodservice, NHS and education sectors.

Having started the business in 2010, Sam and her team have faced some challenging times. These include a recession, and the announcement of Brexit, after which they lost a significant chunk of business. Then Covid-19 hit – something that very few businesses could have foreseen or planned for.

In March 2020, as cases started to rise, orders began to get cancelled. Over 90% of Quattro's orders come from the hospitality and education sector, and with schools all but closed, and hotels and restaurants unable to trade, they were hit hard. Their fridges and freezers were full, but production had almost ground to a halt. Operators stopped paying their bills, and things were beginning to look really worrying.

Quattro also has a contract with *NHS Wales*, along with two small retail contracts for products going into supermarkets. They knew that if they ceased production it could have devastating consequences for these customers, and so it was important that they try and remain operational. Most of the staff were furloughed, but some were kept on to honour these contracts. Sam decided that as they were open, they would also volunteer their services and stock to provide free food for vulnerable people in the community. This kept the remaining staff busy, and avoided having to waste food that would otherwise have perished.

Around this time, Sam received an email from Bicester-based fresh food supplier *Fresh Direct* to say that due to cancelled orders, they were selling off their stock at cost price. Sam replied asking if she could have anything that might be left over afterwards, for the food they were preparing for charity, rather than see it go to waste. *Fresh Direct* later delivered a number of pallets of vegetables, and Quattro's chefs got to work.

An enquiry to Portsmouth City Council asking about appropriate charities resulted in a referral to *HIVE Portsmouth*, and soon they were working with other businesses in the area to source ingredients and produce great food. The food was then delivered to those in need, by volunteers from *Pompey in the Community*.

Solent Butchers, Portsmouth, provided a number of huge smoked hams, which became hearty ham and lentil soup, and *More Food Ltd* bakery in Chichester donated hundreds of premium, hand-make cakes, providing a lovely sweet treat.

Production went on for weeks, and although it was an uncertain and worrying time for the team and they were working flat out, they knew they were doing something amazing for the good of their community. In fact, they adapted brilliantly and remained focused throughout. They also took the opportunity to do lots of development work at this time, including extending their vegan range in preparation for the coming seasons. Sam said "I never cease to be amazed at what Team Quattro achieves, no matter what we're faced with, and I am immensely proud to be part of this team".

June saw Quattro Foods' 10th anniversary – an occasion they'd hoped would be a big celebration. In the end it was a relatively quiet affair with staff socially distanced in the canteen, eating cake and drinking prosecco. Sam hopes to make up for it at some point in the future with a bigger, shinier event!

With the future of the hospitality sector looking so unclear, it's difficult for Sam and her team to plan ahead. After six months of very little income, they've made huge losses, and have only survived thanks to a business loan that they secured in April. Every day is a challenge as they wait to see what will happen next, and their thoughts are with other small businesses, similarly struggling to survive.

> *Sam decided that as they were open, they would also volunteer their services and stock to provide free food for vulnerable people in the community.*

At the time of writing, less than a third of Quattro's pre-Covid business had returned, albeit with a few green shoots of recovery emerging, as more customers planned to return in November.

Sadly, some team members had to be made redundant, as the business simply wasn't able to support them. They were wonderful people, and have been a great loss to the team. The weight of ongoing responsibility that Sam feels to her remaining team of 25 is huge, and she's determined to do everything in her power to stay afloat. Positive and resolute, she knows that the team will continue to pull together, pull through and achieve great things.

Onwards and upwards Sam. With that spirit, you can do anything!

28 Fresh from the Boat – Chantelle & Peter Williams

Chantelle and Peter Williams run award-winning fishmongers 'Fresh from the Boat', selling fresh fish from a number of farm shops and mobile van stalls, plus a new shop at Emsworth Yacht Harbour. It's a family business, with Peter catching the fish and buying fish from other local fisherfolk, and Chantelle selling it. Their aim is simple – to provide local people with sustainable fresh fish at affordable prices.

In November 2019 Chantelle became very ill, and had to undergo major brain surgery. This was followed by five months of rehabilitation, during which time Peter gave up work to look after his wife. They had no money coming in the whole time. It was an extremely difficult time for the family, and Chantelle knew she'd have to return to work much earlier than was recommended.

Their plan was to go back to selling their catch one day a week at *Tuppenny Barn* in Southbourne (Emsworth) to provide them with a small amount of income, and to run the surplus catch to market when needed. Then came the news about Covid-19, and the realisation that the fish markets would have to close. At this point, they went into panic mode, thinking that they wouldn't survive. Sleepless nights ensued, as the only thing they knew was selling fish and other food to their local community.

As the lockdown came into force, the outside world began to resemble a ghost town. With hardly anyone on the roads, and most establishments shut down, and it was a surreal feeling for Peter as he headed out to work.

The couple weren't entitled to any government grants, and were beginning to think that they were doomed, when all of a sudden Chantelle's phone started to ring. And then it rang again, and again – in fact, it didn't stop! It seemed that fresh fish had become like gold dust. 100s of emails and calls a day began flooding in from people wanting fresh fish. Volunteers stepped forward to help them deliver the fish parcels to the community, and they sold a lot of fish – some at cost price to those who couldn't get out, and even giving some away to those who were most in need.

> *The couple weren't entitled to any government grants, and were beginning to think that they were doomed, when all of a sudden Chantelle's phone started to ring.*

The demand for fresh local food had never been so high, and Chantelle's plan to ease herself back into work slowly, went out of the window. They were working up to 100 hours a week at one point to get food out to those who needed it, making sure they supported the regular and loyal customers who'd bought from them for many years.

Chantelle went through a multitude of aprons, gloves and face masks during this time to ensure everyone stayed safe. They were delivering fish to people they never met, by way of a 'no contact' delivery service of knocking, placing the parcels on the doorstep, waving through a window and moving on to the next delivery. Some weeks they supported over 400 families, and it took every last drop of their energy to keep going, leaving them drained at the end of each day. However, they were grateful to be able to serve so many people, who in turn were grateful to receive the fish. The feedback they received was amazing, and made it all worthwhile.

Returning home at the end of 16-20 hour-days and hearing the latest death toll numbers was frightening, as no-one fully understood the risks. On reflection, they're very proud that they were able to keep the service going, and have realised how important it is for the community to have a local fishing vessel for consistent supply.

The new shop is doing well. Whilst the rules are changing almost daily with regard to risk assessments and cleaning regimes, and they've had to adopt a 'one customer in – one customer out' policy, the delivery service has become quieter again.

Chantelle and Peter are grateful to their community for their support and custom during the coronavirus pandemic, and hope that in the months and years to come, many of their new customers will stay with them.

Thank you both for your heroic efforts during such a difficult period personally. Wishing you good health and prosperity now and in the future.

29 GHS Group Ltd – Marc Smith

Marc Smith is the managing partner of Gosport-based GHS Group Ltd, who provide plumbing, heating and electrical services to the commercial and domestic markets. The business is known for its proper, old-fashioned values, and 'Good Honest Service'.

Originally from the Midlands, Marc didn't have a clear idea of what he wanted to do when he left school. A careers computer programme suggested landscape gardening, but he didn't fancy that at the time, so he went to work for ASDA supermarket instead, going on to become their youngest ever manager, and being awarded national 'Manager of the Year'.

At the age of 22, Marc had an epiphany. He didn't want to become a retail robot, and when the government brought in Sunday trading, he wasn't ready to give up his Sunday windsurfing and kitesurfing. He left, and found a job working on a 65ft Swan sailing yacht, spending the next couple of years sailing around Europe, until he was hit by the yacht's boom one day, and broke his shoulder.

Marc found out that day how expendable he was, and returned home to find a more secure job and way of life. He married, started a family, and eventually set up a business partnership with a colleague. This lasted for around a decade, until a reality check one day prompted him to walk away and start again.

He joined his father-in-law's plumbing and heating company in a role focused on business development, and with just a laptop and a phone, he began to bring in new work. In 2015 he finally decided to go solo, launching The GHS Group Ltd.

Marc decided he would set up The GHS Trust to help vulnerable people who couldn't afford to get their boilers fixed.

Marc has always worked hard, but he's also been clear on what was most important to him - protecting his work/life balance and being there for his family. As an example, he's made sure he always attended school sports days, believing that if you can't find two hours out of your life to cheer your children on, there's something wrong. If he's ever had to attend weekend callouts because no-one else has been available, he's found ways of making it up to his family with some kind of a treat the following week.

When lockdown first happened, Marc experienced panic and helplessness as he watched everything he'd worked hard to build up over the years start to disappear. £70,000 worth of purchase orders were cancelled within days, and he was left with just three boiler services in the pipeline.

After a period of time in shock, sitting in his office and wondering what he was going to do next, his survival instinct began to kick in. His staff had all been furloughed at this stage, and he began to think about how he could streamline and develop the business, and use the opportunity to develop his team too. Weekly team *Zoom* calls were set up on a voluntary basis to keep communication and connection going, and everyone turned up. They also ran online social events such as quizzes and an escape room, to help with morale.

A friend had encouraged Marc in the early days of lockdown to "Think like a start-up", taking everything back to basics as if he were starting again from scratch. This gave him a fresh outlook, forcing him to think creatively and innovatively about how he could proceed. He invested in new systems, and began to add content to the business's website and social media channels. This had the effect of reminding people that the business was still there, as well as helping to advise how they could help themselves when they couldn't call an engineer out. Marc's HR manager created some content aimed at apprentices too, offering advice and guidance around presenting themselves professionally when looking for work – all for free. The content was shared widely, helping to raise brand awareness and bring in new enquiries.

A lot of people and charities were struggling financially, and Marc decided he would set up The GHS Trust to help vulnerable people who couldn't afford to get their boilers fixed. He was also able to raise funds for Havant based charity *Music Fusion*, and also to help *Rowner Community Centre* (who were producing ready meals for vulnerable people in Gosport) by fitting a new extraction unit for them free of charge when theirs developed a problem.

As restrictions began to be lifted, business from some clients and contracts started to return – in particular from pubs as they reopened, and also from domestic customers. Things picked up nicely, and Marc believes that he'll look back on lockdown in retrospect and see that it helped to transform and benefit his business.

The lockdown period also caused Marc to reflect on his homelife. He realised that, whilst he had a beautiful home, it wasn't well designed for home working and schooling. His children had actually adapted well in the circumstances, and he was proud of how hard they worked. He decided to convert some space upstairs into a proper study area for them, and he also built a home office for himself on a bit of land at the bottom of his garden, with some help from a friend. They are all set up for the future now, should anything like lockdown happen again.

As the saying goes, lockdown showed Marc that when life presents you with lemons, you can choose to make lemonade. He believes there's no point in feeling sorry for yourself – that you have to look for the opportunities instead, and be prepared to start again from the basics. In his own words, "Gear up, and stay fluid".

That sounds like good, honest advice to us!

30 The Queens Hotel - Farid Yeganeh

The Queens Hotel, in the heart of Southsea, may have had to close their doors to regular business during the early lockdown period, but 'lockdown' definitely wasn't a case of 'shutdown'. Managing Director Farid Yeganeh was proud to offer respite and solace to NHS frontline workers during the crisis.

Nurse Gemma Powell lived at the Queens Hotel for nearly two months whilst caring for patients on the *Respiratory High Care* ward at *Queen Alexandra Hospital*. She couldn't go home as the ward was a high-risk environment, and her pregnant daughter was in the higher risk category.

Gemma said "I will never forget how well we were treated at the Queens Hotel – I've never felt so special. It is a beautiful building and the staff are amazing - they are like family. I would get in from a night shift and everything would be clean and perfect in the room - there would be goodies waiting for me and even a card, which made me cry. If ever I was exhausted emotionally, the staff at the hotel would cheer me up. If I could have brought my daughter and cat to live with me, I would have stayed there forever."

Seeing the NHS workers returning exhausted to the hotel, kind-hearted Duty Manager Megan Lockyer came up with the idea of making up hampers for them. "The NHS staff had told us how sore their hands were due to constant washing, and we were able to include aloe vera hand cream along with face masks, relaxing bath gels, slippers, and other items," she explained.

During this time, MD Farid joined forces with General Manager Chris Gilmore, Head Chef Paul Playford from sister hotel the *Royal Beach*, and Brasserie Blanc's Niko Nedelcu, to create up to 600 delicious hot meals every week in the hotel's kitchen, for the city's vulnerable residents.

Niko's son Sheylan has Down's syndrome, and spent his first year in hospital following heart reconstruction surgery. Sheylan turned six in July, and Niko believes he owes the NHS everything. "We've made donations and supported charity events since my son's birth, and I saw the opportunity to cook for vulnerable people and nursing staff as a great way to give something back", he said.

Thousands of pounds were donated by city-based companies including *PMC Construction*, along with food from suppliers such as local butcher *Buckwells of Southsea*. The meals were delivered by Clare Martin's team at *Pompey in the Community*, in association with *HIVE Portsmouth*. CEO Clare said "The meals prepared at the Queens Hotel were really special, and receiving one was such a treat. One person burst into tears when our volunteer arrived with food for them, they were so delighted."

In recent years the hotel has undergone a massive refurbishment, restoring it to its original glory. Many rooms have spectacular sea views, and facilities include bars, a restaurant, and a large private garden hosting music events in the summer months. The hotel is the perfect setting for business events, weddings and special occasions. A luxury spa is in the pipeline, coming soon.

Whilst it's difficult to plan for the future, one thing is for sure – The Queens Hotel in Southsea will continue to find ways of serving and delighting customers for many years to come.

31 SC Vital Fitness – Sean Cole

Sean Cole, a former Royal Navy physical training instructor and father of two, is the director of SC Vital Fitness in Drayton, Portsmouth – a small, independent gym offering personal training services.

Fitness has been a passion for Sean for as long as he can remember. As a boy, he was always full of energy and never sat still, and that's still very much the case today!

At the age of 30, Sean went back to university and gained his Certificate in Further Education and Training (Cert Ed). A few years later, he went back again to do a master's degree in Strength & Conditioning Science, and is now an accredited coach with the UK Strength & Conditioning Association, specialising in injury rehabilitation.

In February 2020 the gym was fully refurbished, and the team were looking forward to a bumper year. However, on 21st March, just before the formal lockdown, gyms of all sizes in the UK were instructed to cease trading. It was a stressful and frustrating time for Sean. Worrying about his business, his staff and the many customers who were being made redundant had an impact on his mental health. Whilst he could understand the decision in respect of large commercial gyms where there's sometimes very little distance between apparatus, he felt that small gyms like his own could operate safely by zoning off areas and putting in place stringent hygiene measures. He even gathered a petition of 3000 signatures to appeal to the government to rethink the sanctions.

Sean contacted these members and offered them the online package free of charge…

With his team all furloughed, Sean focused on doing the only thing he could think of to ensure continuity of service to his customers, and that was to set up online training and coaching sessions via *Zoom*. He got a digital camera set up, and from there on, in his own words, did his best *Joe Wicks* impression, broadcasting live in the early morning and evenings!

Sean slashed membership fees by more than half to reflect the reduction in service, but a lot of members dropped out due to redundancy and financial pressures. Upset because he knew it wasn't their fault, Sean contacted these members and offered them the online package free of charge, as well as the loan of equipment that they could use as part of the workouts. He knew that, not only would the online training help his customers with their mental health, it was also helping him with his own. He even lost weight, he was jumping around so much – around 6 kilos in all!

In early June he was able to bring a few of his team members back in again on a part-time basis, and they expanded their online offering. It wasn't all rosy – some days were really hard, and Sean, who's normally a very upbeat, positive character, struggled to see the light at the end of the tunnel. However, the team were brilliant, and helped him to stay focused. Eventually, 500 *Zoom* sessions, 1,200 phone calls and 60 outdoor sessions later, the light reappeared, and on 25th July they were able to open their doors once again, with a few changes.

Since then, the business has been doing well. They've had new customers through the doors, and it's looking like they might begin to break even again by September or October, by which time Sean hopes that all of his staff will be back full-time.

He's very grateful to his team and to the business's loyal members, all of whom have been unwavering in their support. Without them he doubts SC Vital Fitness would still be here, and he can't thank everyone enough for the fighting chance they've given the business.

Sean hopes to employ more coaches and trainers in the future, in order to help even more people with their fitness journeys. When customers join the gym, they get a quality personal service from highly trained professionals, along with a strong community of support where everyone can rise together.

With such a worthy aim and ambition, Sean, we wish you every success!

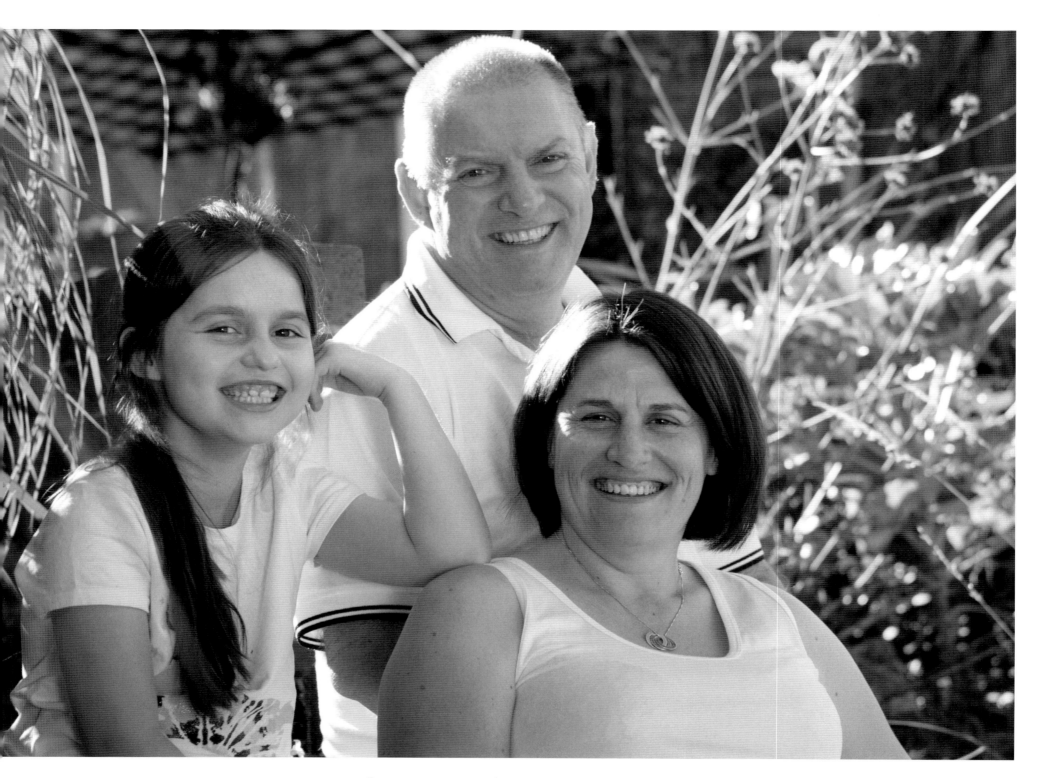

32 A1 Print Services Ltd – David MacAskill

Dave MacAskill is a former teacher from Waterlooville who set up his printing and merchandise company, A1 Print Services Ltd, in 2018.

When Covid-19 struck, his business was one of many which didn't qualify for financial help under any of the government's business support schemes.

With all of Dave's work disappearing overnight, a home to maintain and a wife and child to support, panic set in. There was nothing else for it – he had to look for work quickly, at a time when jobs were scarce. Being the resourceful type, he found two jobs within a short space of time. The first job was stacking shelves at *Tesco* two nights a week, which was hard, physical work. The second was a contract with *Morrisons* for 10 hours a week (often creeping up to 24), where his responsibilities included stacking shelves, marshalling duties, and working on the tills.

He also set up a crowd-funding campaign to raise additional funds, managing to hit his target of £5,000 within 46 days, receiving a match-funded donation from the *Solent Local Enterprise Partnership* (LEP). Dave gave half of all donations received to other causes, helping to furnish a single parent's first home, and also donating furniture to the *Moving On* project in Portsmouth.

In between supermarket shifts, Dave carried out a number of charitable acts, including:
- producing clothing to raise funds for the Falklands Veteran Foundation
- donating items to Emsworth charity Verity's Gift
- producing thank you cards for *HIVE Portsmouth*, to thank everyone who'd helped them during lockdown
- laser-engraving mask clips for nurses at Queen Alexandra Hospital
- producing merchandise and print for The Parenting Network.

2020 had looked set to be an excellent year for the business. Dave had a number of events lined up which he'd invested time, money and effort into, and which had to be cancelled due to the virus. The first was *HMS Queen Elizabeth's* 'Freedom of Entry' parade in March at Wantage (the birthplace of *King Alfred*, who's thought to have founded The Navy in the 9th century). With an estimated 50,000 visitors due to attend, Dave had produced a large number of collectors' military coin sets that, if they'd all sold, would have generated around £200,000. He's since managed to sell only a small percentage of these personally and online at www.hmsstores.co.uk

The next cancellation was the *Portsmouth Business Expo* in April, which he'd been organising with director Gary Dickens for over six months. Finally, there was the *Chilli & Gin Festival* in May, with 80 stallholders booked and 18 bands due to play over two days – the first of its kind in Portsmouth. His business partner Mark Scarborough had grown 3500 chilli plants in preparation for the festival. They managed to sell 800 plants privately, and the rest, heartbreakingly, had to be destroyed – albeit recycled into compost for the following year.

Whilst it was a difficult year which held a lot of challenges and disappointments, Dave invested his energy into doing everything he could to stay afloat, whilst also helping others that needed some help. Thankfully, business began to pick up in the summer months, and he's hoping 2021 will more than make up for 2020's losses.

Dave gave half of all donations received to other causes, helping to furnish a single parent's first home, and also donating furniture to the Moving On project in Portsmouth.

Looking ahead, Dave is currently exploring the feasibility of establishing a training facility in Portsmouth's dockyard. The aim is to offer disadvantaged young people apprenticeships in retail and manufacturing. It would also support veterans and military spouses in the transition into civilian life, and jobs within the tourist industry. One thing's for sure – he's not going to the let the grass grow under his feet!

Dave, your service to others at a time when you were personally struggling is inspirational. You are a survivor and a true gentleman.

33 Unlocking Potential – Gethin Jones

Gethin Jones is a leadership development consultant, inspirational speaker, coach and author of the book 'Unconscious Incarceration'.

When the country went into lockdown, Gethin was somewhat ahead of the curve, having had prior experience of losing his freedom and liberty as a prisoner within the criminal justice system.

Gethin had been sensitive as a young boy, and remembers feeling like a lost soul – disconnected from his family. He was placed in and out of care a number of times growing up, was expelled from school at the age 11, and struggled to manage his emotions and behaviours. By the time he was in his teenage years he was considered beyond parental control, and at the age of 14 he was sentenced to the short, sharp shock of a juvenile detention centre, in the hope that he would be 'scared straight'. It didn't work, and he was in and out of prison a number of times over the next two decades, developing a drug dependency, and spending a total of eight years behind prison doors.

At the age of 34 he made the decision to change, and in the years since, he has educated and developed himself to such an extent that he now educates and inspires others, in both the criminal justice system and the corporate world.

When the lockdown came into force, Gethin knew that the best response would be to accept the situation quickly, and create a new routine for himself. Over the previous few years, he'd travelled the length and breadth of the UK, always on the road and staying in hotels. It wasn't the healthiest of lifestyles. When he wasn't on the road, he would spend his time networking, and then one day in March it all ended, and he was left wondering what on earth he was going to do with his time.

Having learned the skills of constructive thinking through his years of self-development, one of the first things Gethin decided to do was to get fit. As he was having some landscaping done to his garden at the time, he decided to make use of the equipment around him, and constructed a makeshift gym out of wheelbarrows, bricks, and other building materials.

He also decided to tackle his nutrition, and invested in *HelloFresh* recipe boxes to ensure he was getting a healthy, balanced diet. Eating well, using fresh ingredients, helped him to feel good mentally as well as physically.

Gethin spent a lot of time reading and listening to audio books and podcasts throughout lockdown, particularly the work of self-development and spiritual author Dr Wayne Dyer. He also scaled back on the amount of time he found himself spending on social media, recognising that all the scrolling and comparing he was doing wasn't helping his mental health.

These activities provided Gethin with an excellent foundation of well-being from which to plan his next steps.

When *Highbury College* got in touch to ask if he'd record a video for their students, Gethin was more than happy to oblige. From this, he came up with the idea of recording a series of 'An Interview With…' themed videos, where he would interview former prisoners like himself, enabling them to share their stories, describing their experiences of life before, during and after being incarcerated. His vision was that these videos would be played in prisons across the UK, providing hope and inspiration for the residents.

Gethin created a crowdfunding campaign to fund ten video interviews, raising over £16,000 in the process. He worked with videographer Bill Moulsdale of *Giant Leap Video & Photography* to record the interviews via *Zoom*. The videos were transferred to DVD, and to date, 56 prisons have requested copies.

In addition, Gethin also wrote eight articles for a weekly prison newsletter with a reach of 90,000 potential readers, and since then he's been asked to do more. His aim is to initiate hope, and show that change is possible if prisoners engage with the services and support available to them (but for which there's sometimes mistrust).

One of his next missions will be to create an online learning platform with training programmes for those serving community sentences, to help them to move forward with their lives.

Gethin is a busy man. He has meetings in the pipeline with the *Ministry of Justice* to discuss the redesign of the probation service, and also with Prisons Minister, Lucy Frazer QC. His voice is being heard, and he is having an influence on decisions that are being made.

On a personal level, he completed the *National Three Peaks Challenge* in October, climbing the three highest peaks in England, Scotland and Wales and performing one of his trademark headstands at the top of each peak. In doing so, he raised over £2,000 for the *Flying Solo* www.flyingsolo.org.uk/ charity that provides opportunities for Portsmouth www.hampshirelive.news/all-about/portsmouth care leavers. He hopes his efforts will gain him a place in the *Guinness Book of Records*!

One of his next missions will be to create an online learning platform with training programmes for those serving community sentences, to help them to move forward with their lives.

Gethin's favourite memory from the early days of the lockdown is of the complete peace and quiet that could be found on the seafront. The sea was crystal clear, and the skies were clear, too. There were very few people around, and he finally felt a sense of connection with the world that had always felt missing.

The time provided Gethin with an opportunity to reflect on his life – what he'd been doing, and where he was going. He's very keen to remember those early reflections, so he can take the learning with him into the future as the world begins to speed up again.

Gethin's mantra is "Think it, Say it, Do it!". His book 'Unconscious Incarceration' can be purchased online at www.amazon.co.uk

34 Koop+Kraft Restaurant – George Purnell

George Purnell is the owner and manager of Koop+Kraft restaurant in Cowplain, Waterlooville, which first opened for business in January 2018.

As an 18-year-old Business Studies student, George found a part-time job in Clanfield restaurant *Kassia*. At the time it was a means to an end, and he hadn't anticipated that the industry would grab him in the way that it did. However, he soon discovered that he loved it, and found an excellent mentor in business owner and entrepreneur Kaz Miah, whom he later helped to launch a number of other successful restaurants in the area.

By the age of 24, and having learned a lot from Kaz, George had begun to want something more. He decided it was time to start making his own decisions. Highly ambitious and driven, he wanted his own restaurant, but felt that fine dining wasn't really for him. He had the idea of theming his restaurant around fried chicken, as he found it such a satisfying and comforting food, and something of a guilty pleasure!

When he was 25, he opened the doors of Koop+Kraft – a restaurant born out of his passion for reinventing comfort food, and it's been a tough but rewarding journey ever since. His first year of trading was OK, but the second year was much better. Being someone that doesn't like to sit still for long, in February of 2020 he was making big plans for the business, looking ahead to what they would do for the various upcoming holidays and events.

By March, the situation with Covid-19 was becoming serious, and the government began advising people in vulnerable categories to avoid confined spaces such as pubs and restaurants. Although this was worrying for the business, George hoped that, even if restaurants were told to close, they would be able to continue trading as a take-away. Mother's Day was coming up and he wanted to donate some meals to NHS workers at *Queen Alexandra Hospital*, so he decided to go ahead and put in his usual food delivery order, plus some extras for the NHS.

When the food delivery didn't turn up the next day, a phone call revealed that the suppliers had run out of stock due to people panic buying. George decided to drive to the wholesalers himself the following morning at 7am to miss the crowds, but when he got there it was as busy and frantic as Black Friday, and he still couldn't get everything he wanted.

On Friday 20th March, after a really busy shift, Koop+Kraft decided to close the restaurant's doors. The next day, the business began operating solely as a take-away delivery service. That weekend they donated 150 take-aways to the *Queen Alexandra Hospital*, and ran a delivery service for Mother's Day roast dinners. The team worked extremely hard, and the weekend was a big success.

Monday 23rd March was an anxious day for all concerned, as the country awaited a formal government statement on the coronavirus. At this stage, no-one knew specifically what the worsening situation would mean, either for people and their freedoms, or businesses and their ability to continue trading. That evening, as well as instructing people to stay at home, Prime Minister Boris Johnson also encouraged the use of food delivery services.

This was the official 'Go-ahead' that George and the team had hoped they'd get. When he'd asked individual team members if they'd wanted to join him in working through, they all opted in, believing it would be better for their mental health and well-being to be busy, rather than laid off.

As it turned out, the team ended up doing double the amount of business that they'd anticipated. It had been a once-in-a-lifetime opportunity. The big fast-food chains had closed down, and it was all a bit surreal.

They team loved the empty roads and supermarkets during this time, although sourcing all the stock they needed was a challenge. Supermarkets were rationing certain items, and they were having to make multiple trips to source enough burger buns. Everyone rose to the occasion though, and it was a massive team effort.

George is extremely grateful to his team and his customers for their support throughout. He received many lovely messages of support after posting his weekly updates online, and it was clear how much people appreciated being able to get their Friday or Saturday night take-aways.

That weekend they donated 150 take-aways to the Queen Alexandra Hospital, and ran a delivery service for Mother's Day roast dinners.

As good as business had been, George had worked liked a trojan, and the situation took a lot out of him over the spring and summer months. He was grateful when things slowed down a little, and whilst he'd like to be able to make some firm plans, the future is still looking unclear. For now though, he's happy to tread water, and will continue doing whatever he can to keep the business going and keep his loyal customers fed and happy! At some point he may well consider opening a second restaurant, but for the moment, it's 'business as unusual'!

Good call George. We know that when the time's right, there'll be no stopping you!

35

Luxury Gift in a Box – Rhona Rogers & Jacquie Fitton

Business partners Rhona Rogers and Jacquie Fitton launched their business, Luxury Gift in a Box, a few weeks before the lockdown.

The pair had started selling goods on Amazon the previous year, before taking the decision to future-proof their business by setting up their own branded website in addition.

With no formal training, they created their website, and prepared themselves for what they thought would be a soft start. However, from that very first day they've hardly stopped. They soon had a portfolio of 30+ gift sets (and growing) for all occasions, ranging from pampering goods, to candles, reed diffusers, new baby gifts, journaling sets, and more.

With most shops being shut, sales of goods online (already a growing market pre-lockdown) flourished even more – especially the market for gifts and treats. Gifting seemed to became more frequent in lockdown too, with people wanting to thank others for the acts of kindness that were commonplace during this time, and also to remind relatives and friends that they loved them and were thinking about them.

Rhona and Jacquie were able to continue working through the crisis. Despite being so busy (and missing out on some of the beautiful weather which was a feature of the early days of the lockdown), they were thrilled to be doing their bit to brighten up people's lives, knowing that their gorgeous gifts were making a difference.

Whilst they weren't on the front-line, they were providing what felt like a vital service – helping people to enjoy their special days, and providing others with a way of saying "Thank you" that felt more tangible, and held more meaning, than words alone.

Rhona and Jacquie's gifts are more special than deliveries from many larger businesses, because the items are selected and packaged with care, attention and thought as to how the person receiving the gift will feel when they open it. It's all done with love, and they believe that customers will feel the difference.

The future's looking bright for this energetic duo, who are now looking ahead to the Christmas market. They are making contact with small, artisan producers and suppliers of sustainable, environmentally friendly gifts and packaging which everyone can feel good about.

Wishing you both all the very best.

36 Emily Alexander - Entrepreneur

In March 2020, Emily Alexander, a project/event support freelancer and entrepreneur from Portsmouth, took the decision to come off anti-depressants after taking them for 10 years. She'd worked hard over the previous years to develop her resilience and coping skills, and felt the time was right to face life unmedicated.

EMILY ALEXANDER - ENTREPRENEUR

When the lockdown came into force, all of Emily's work was cancelled. As a new small business, she wasn't eligible for any of the government's financial support schemes, and the situation was extremely worrying. Emily went through a very difficult few weeks, battling the strong pull she was feeling to fall back into anxiety and panic about how she, her husband and their five cats would survive.

Recognising that she'd need some support to get through this time, she sought the help of a mental health coach, and began to focus instead on ways she could help others. With paid work looking unlikely for the foreseeable future, and with time on her hands, Emily decided that she would look for ways to bring a bit of happiness and joy into people's lives, to counteract all the doom and gloom.

When she heard that *HIVE Portsmouth* were looking for volunteers for their *Covid Response Team*, Emily got in touch straight away. They needed people to assist with leaflet distribution, collecting and delivering prescriptions and food, befriending people and making welfare checks. Emily delivered over 1000 leaflets for *HIVE*, advising recipients of how and where they could get help if they were self-isolating or shielding.

Another group looking for volunteers was the *Portsmouth Coronavirus Support Group*, set up to provide a network of helpers to support those who were self-isolating or at risk. Emily joined them as a volunteer, and enjoyed brightening up local open spaces and parks where people would take their daily exercise, with colourful pinwheels, butterflies and wishing wands. After years of her life revolving around work objectives and deadlines, and never having the time to sit and catch up with herself, Emily really enjoyed getting in touch with her creative side once again. She particularly loved seeing the smiles on people's faces when they caught sight of the bright colours.

Emily also took up singing lessons during lockdown, and joined a virtual choir set up by the *ExcludedUK* group. The group is an alliance of freelancers and small business owners from the community of three million who weren't eligible for government financial support – many of whom have experienced hardship and even mental ill-health as a result.

In July, as a number of businesses and organisations began the process of reviews, restructures and redundancies, Emily was moved to hear about the number of expected redundancies. Given her experience in HR and careers mentoring, she set up the *Facebook* page 'Redundancy Support UK', bringing together a network of professionals offering a broader support package. This included legal advice, money advice, mental health support and career path exploration, amongst other services.

> *When she heard that HIVE Portsmouth were looking for volunteers for their Covid Response Team, Emily got in touch straight away. They needed people to assist with leaflet distribution, collecting and delivering prescriptions and food, befriending people and making welfare checks.*

Emily was able, through the lockdown, to turn a difficult personal situation into an opportunity to connect with, and help, other people. She learnt that well-being should come before anything else in life, and that when we connect with, and give to others, it supports our own well-being too.

Emily hopes it won't be too long until her project/event support work (Pair of Hands Business Services) is in full swing once again, and her cat-sitting side-line (Purrfect-Company) can resume.

Whatever the future holds for Emily, we feel sure it will be bright and colourful!

37 The Aroma Studios - Nicky Jones

Nicky is an aromatherapist and skincare specialist from Warsash. She'd struggled with eczema and dermatitis all her life, before discovering a natural skincare brand in 2013 which cleared up her skin almost overnight.

Nicky realised that her skin didn't respond well to chemicals, detergents and synthetic perfumes, and when she swapped these things for natural, organic products, everything changed. It was so transformative that she became a sales consultant for the brand, and started to learn more about skincare.

In 2016 she trained as a complementary therapist, studying anatomy, physiology, reflexology, massage and aromatherapy. Once finished, and hungry for more learning, Nicky set up her business, The Aroma Studio, and jumped straight into a Level 4 diploma in clinical aromatherapy. Having completed her diploma, and feeling like she was done with studying, Nicky focused full time on her business, where she specialises in aromatherapy and reflexology. She also began making her own soaps and body products.

Business grew steadily, and so did the product range. In 2019, Nicky caught the learning bug once again, and completed a course in bespoke skincare, before feeling the urge to take this learning further, and signing up for a diploma in organic skincare formulation in January 2020. Shortly afterwards, the country went into lockdown.

> *Nicky developed four formulations (Balance, Focus, Calm and Boost), and created a 'Buy one, Give one' scheme where for every item she sold, she donated another to frontline workers at Southampton General Hospital.*

Not being able to see clients one-to-one, Nicky decided to focus on her diploma, and on developing new aromatherapy products to support her clients. This included the addition of pulse-point roll-on oils, which were probably the biggest hit of lockdown. Nicky developed four formulations (Balance, Focus, Calm and Boost), and created a 'Buy one, Give one' scheme where for every item she sold, she donated another to frontline workers at *Southampton General Hospital*. Nicky received reports from the *Intensive Care Unit* that the some of the roll-on oils were placed on the *Personal Protective Equipment* (PPE) stations where nursing staff gowned and masked up before going on duty. The workers were loving using them, saying that the oils were helping them to feel less anxious.

Nicky loves her work, in particular the bespoke side of what she does – mixing up completely natural potions that meet the exact skincare and emotional requirements of her clients.

What a wonderful service!

38 Gunwharf Quays (Landsec)

Gunwharf Quays in Portsmouth is the south coast's leading designer outlet shopping centre, and home to over 90 stores plus a cinema, bowling alley and over 30 restaurants, bars and cafes. When the lockdown was introduced, the majority of the centre's stores had to close, and the usually busy and bustling environment became unusually peaceful.

The surrounding landscape blossomed as Spring burst into life, and the coastal air and sea appeared fresher and cleaner than ever.

Shops providing essential items, such as *Tesco* and *Boots the Chemist* remained open, providing great service to customers throughout. Lots of planning went into the creation of one-way systems, signage, hand sanitising stations, and so on, and safety was a priority. Cleaning, security and the technical teams remained in post, but the majority of the centre's workers worked from home or were furloughed.

Gunwharf Quays' management team secured funding from its owner, Landsec, for its partner charity, *Pompey in the Community*, who, in association with *HIVE Portsmouth,* provided food parcels to the most vulnerable in the community. Gunwharf Quays was also able to donate food items such as chocolate Easter eggs from the Lindt store, as well as bags from *Le Creuset*, *Denby* and *Radley* to help get the food packaged up for a week's worth of supplies.

Whilst a few brands very sadly went into administration through the lockdown period, the vast majority survived. Once restrictions eased and stores were able to re-open (with relevant safety measures in place, and limited capacity), shoppers began to return. Most customers have been really thankful for the centre's commitment to safety, and haven't minded the queuing that has sometimes been necessary.

Whilst online shopping was a blessing through lockdown, nothing can quite beat the experience of a day out to a centre like Gunwharf Quays, where you can wander around at your leisure and take in all the sights, sounds, smells, tastes and textures.

Landsec's Assistant Centre Director, Yvonne Clay said "We are very proud to be one of the biggest employers in the city, and we know how important Gunwharf Quays is for the people of Portsmouth. As such, it's been incredibly positive to see our brand partners reopen, to see so many customers coming back to visit, and to have received a huge amount of positive feedback. We can't thank the people of Portsmouth enough for their support, and for abiding by our new safety measures to help keep all of us as safe as possible."

Gunwharf Quays is a wonderful and much-loved asset to the city and local landscape. Many thanks to all concerned for a fantastic effort through the Covid crisis. Long may you thrive!

39 Joe Tyler - Blacksmith

Joe Tyler is a blacksmith from Hampshire who graduated from the *National School of Blacksmithing* in Hereford in 2012, following a three-year course. Prior to this, he'd been a tree-worker, and had become interested in blacksmithing through his love of early Saxon historical re-enactments.

Since qualifying, Joe has balanced self-employment as a blacksmith, with teaching the craft to others – firstly at *Chichester College*, and in recent years, at *Plumpton Agricultural College* near Brighton.

When the lockdown came into force, Joe's teaching work was moved online. Luckily, he has his own portable work kit, and was able to continue with most of his blacksmithing work. In fact, lockdown was a highly creative time for him, and he enjoyed experimenting with all sorts of items, from gates and railings, to garden sculptures, furniture, jewellery – even making faces made out of sheet metal.

Joe gets bored if he doesn't have enough to do, so he kept himself busy throughout the year. He's active on *Instagram* (joethesmithy), where you can find many striking images of his work. Inspired by others working in similar ancient crafts (notably, flint knapper and Stone age crafts expert, Will Lord), he decided to have a go at making some videos of himself engaged in his craft. He asked people for ideas of what they'd like to see him make, and he had fun with this, demonstrating that the lockdown didn't have to be all doom and gloom. A key message was that a great way to get through a difficult time is to keep busy, finding creative things to do or make. A friend composed some music for the videos, and they're in the process of developing a YouTube channel where they can post them.

Joe's a fan of upcycling, and when the tips and recycling centres closed, he put a post on a *Horndean and Clanfield Facebook page* asking if anyone had any old metal he could collect, to use in upcycling projects, including a commemorative sculpture that he was planning. He received a steady amount of donations from this, and many of the donors kept in contact, interested to see the outcome of the projects.

Joe joined forces with blacksmithing friends Jade Smith *Instagram* username *blacksmithjade* (seen in the photograph), and David Mortimer of *Firebird Forge*, to arrange a collaboration between 12 blacksmiths, who would work individually to create panels for two commemorative benches to mark the lockdown. The plan is for the blacksmiths to make a panel each, and the panels will then be brought together to form the benches. Whilst the location for the finished articles hasn't yet been confirmed, the plan is place them side by side, but two metres apart – replicating the distancing that was required in the early days of lockdown. Work on the project has been paused temporarily, as a film company are interested in filming the process, but restrictions have made this difficult for them. Joe's hope it won't be too long before the project can resume.

Joe and Jade are also planning to collaborate on a sculpture in recognition of NHS workers' bravery and care throughout the pandemic. The details of this have yet to be agreed, and work is likely to commence in early 2021.

It's been a year of dreaming and planning as well as experimenting, and Joe's been in discussions with a team of blacksmiths to create a themed touring event/entertainment spectacle where they'll be able to bring people together to promote the craft of blacksmithing, as well as the upcycling of materials. Those involved will dress up to tie in with the theme, and visitors will be able to watch displays, and have a go at making things themselves. The events are likely to be a year and a half in development, so for the time being, they are collecting materials and ideas, ready for the time when events are able to take place again.

Joe is thankful for the extra time that the lockdown provided him with, to get creative and plan these projects – ideas that, in other circumstances, might not have made it onto the drawing board. He believes that, in the push to achieve a standard of living, we'd lost our quality of life, becoming so time poor that we had little scope or energy for expressing our creative tendencies. What the virus gave us was time, and he noticed that more and more people were starting to do things with their hands.

He also noticed that people seemed to be turning away from 'cheap and cheerful' mass-produced items, and supporting local craftsmen and women instead, investing in hand-crafted items that would last for many years. Joe believes that the movement towards all things 'local' will grow, and that after many of wanting everything bigger, faster and cheaper, the tables have turned.

Joe's aim is not only to promote the art of blacksmithing, but also to develop the craft, and raise the bar for the industry. He's been liaising with *Havant and South Downs College* in connection with offering work experience opportunities to their art and design students, and hopes this is something that can be trialled in 2021.

Joe, with your active, creative mind, and your energy for getting things done, we suspect there's nothing that you couldn't achieve!

ENTERTAINMENT STORIES

Much of the entertainment industry in the UK and across the globe was unable to operate during the crisis, leaving many entertainment professionals out of work, and many people wondering how they were going to keep themselves and their families amused.

Live music, festivals, fun-parks, events of all kinds, sport, theatre, cinema, dancing, and so on, were either cancelled, closed, postponed, or in some cases, taken online. This included a number of live-streamed concerts by well-known music artists such as *Take That*, *Coldplay's Chris Martin*, and *Lady Gaga*, whose 'One World: Together at Home' concert raised funds for frontline healthcare workers and the *World Health Organisation*.

Many museums and galleries offered free virtual tours; some zoos had live webcams; and concert halls offered live streaming.

There was a surge in TV watching and online streaming, with adults reportedly spending an average of six hours 25 minutes a day staring at screens, during the height of lockdown. Eight out of ten people in the UK admitted to spending meaningless time scrolling on social media – an activity known to have a negative impact on mental health, self-esteem and sleep patterns. *Netflix* documentary 'The Social Dilemma' was released in September, highlighting the addictive nature of platforms such as *Facebook* and *Instagram*, which seek to keep users' attention for as long as possible, as often as possible. The documentary caused many to reflect on their habits, and those of their children, suggesting a correlation between social media use and a sharp increase in suicide deaths amongst young girls.

Video-sharing entertainment platform *Tiktok* was the most down-loaded app of the period, with 315 million downloads worldwide in the first quarter of 2020 alone. Usage skyrocketed, with adults getting in on the act as well as young people, creating comedy sketches as well as singing and dancing videos.

There were stories in the media of care homes playing 'doorway bingo' with residents seated in the doorways of their rooms, facing out into the corridors where someone called the numbers. Later on, when restrictions began to lift and weather allowed, some care home residents enjoyed garden concerts.

We learnt that we didn't always need to go out and spend money to amuse ourselves, and that activities at home with our families could be fun. Pre-lockdown, a lot of entertainment had been rather passive, but it became more active, as we were forced to create fun for ourselves. Many played games and created online quizzes for family and friends – often with alcohol to replicate a pub quiz! Socially-distanced picnics were also popular.

Many musicians took to singing and playing on their doorsteps or balconies to entertain their neighbours. Here are just a few stories from some of Hampshire's shining stars, who helped to brighten up our days in lockdown.

40

Robbie James - Express FM

Radio is a comforting, reliable medium of communication that's been informing, entertaining and helping people to feel connected since the year 1900. The medium seemed to become even more important during lockdown, with people seemingly needing the company and upliftment more than ever.

Robbie James is a freelance radio DJ, stadium presenter and event host from Bishops Waltham. He got into student radio when studying economics in Edinburgh, and fell in love with it. He also completed an internship for *Capital FM* in the city, before heading back to the south coast.

Robbie – a huge cricket fan and former player for Hampshire's junior squad – began presenting at Portsmouth radio station *Express FM* in 2018, and was due to move on in April 2020 to take up a stadium presenter contract at the *Ageas Bowl* cricket ground. However, when the country went into lockdown in March, competitive cricket went into shutdown, and plans were delayed.

Robbie was thrilled to be able to stay on at *Express FM*, presenting the music, fun and entertainment-based *Drivetime* show on weekdays. He also presented the more informative and talk-based 'Coronavirus Specials' on Wednesday evenings, which focused on local coronavirus news and statistics. These commitments enabled him to keep busy, supporting and entertaining local people through the difficult time.

Robbie is also a proud ambassador for *Naomi House* and *Jacksplace* (hospices for children and young people near Winchester), and hosts all their fundraising events. During lockdown, all scheduled events had to be cancelled and their charity shops closed, creating a difficult situation for them financially. However, Robbie was able to host a number of virtual fundraising quizzes for the charity via *Facebook Live*, raising up to £1,000 on each occasion.

As an energetic and motivated person who likes to feel that he's making consistent progress in life, Robbie could have felt very frustrated and disappointed that the virus had seemingly put a halt on his plans. Instead, he chose to channel his energy into entertaining people and helping good causes. He described the lockdown period as a "mad but magical time" when rather than losing out, new opportunities opened up for him.

Many thanks to Robbie and the team at *Express FM* for doing such a sterling job of keeping their listeners informed, entertained and uplifted.

All the best, Robbie, for your future plans and adventures.

41
Amy Baker

Amy Baker is a jazz and swing singer with a vintage 1950s vibe, who lives in Southsea.

When the country first went into lockdown, Amy experienced a range of difficult emotions including panic, anger, fear and disappointment, as all her summer concerts, events and her first international festival as an artist in her own right were being cancelled.

She was also due to marry her fiancé in a lavish ceremony in July, and it felt as though all her hopes and plans for the year were being dashed.

Being a generally positive person, it didn't take too long before she managed to shift her perspective, accept the situation, and look for something positive to do.

As well as decorating her home, Amy has also:
- arranged a *VE Day* 75th anniversary celebration party and commemorative gig for the residents of her road, where her rendition of *Dame Vera Lynn's* 'We'll Meet Again' went down a storm
- performed a number of free online gigs via *Facebook Live* on Mondays, Wednesdays & Fridays
- sung for the residents and staff of a care home in Fareham, in their gardens
- performed singing telegrams by video for friends, family and others, who were thrilled to get personal messages and songs for their special occasions.

Amy was able to reach a far wider audience than ever before, having people from America, Italy, Sweden and elsewhere tuning in to her online gigs, and she was inundated with kindness, support and messages of thanks. She confessed that she'd enjoyed her time during lockdown, discovering that she was very happy to be at home with her fiancé and her dog, in bare feet rather than high heels!

When the country first went into lockdown, Amy experienced a range of difficult emotions including panic, anger, fear and disappointment, as all her summer concerts, events and her first international festival as an artist in her own right were being cancelled.

The couple chose to marry in a small ceremony at the local registry office in July, and are looking forward to holding a big reception party in 2021.

Many congratulations to you both, and wishing you many years of bliss and harmony!

42

Aled Price

Aled Price is an entertainments director and professional performer from Milton with a background in musical theatre and teaching, and a passion for making the arts inclusive and accessible to all. He runs Aled Price Productions, supplying entertainment and tribute acts to hotels, pubs and clubs, and also for events and parties. He also runs two theatre schools, in Havant and in Milton.

Aled's mission and motto through lockdown has been to 'SPREAD THE JOY'. As part of this mission, he has:

- run through the streets of Portsmouth in full *Spiderman* costume a number of times, as part of his daily exercise. He posted videos of these runs to the *Keep Milton Green Facebook* page, and was met by lots of people clapping, waving and cheering. He particularly loved talking to the children, encouraging them to take up the mission of looking after their grown-ups at home!
- organised a socially distanced street party for his road where everyone came together and got to know one another better as people, rather than 'passing ships'
- shopped and dropped off 120 food deliveries on his bike to those who weren't able to go out themselves – even managing to source eggs when all the supermarkets had run out.

Aled has found the Milton community to be incredibly loving and supportive, with lots of residents helping each other out by dropping food off to vulnerable people, providing lifts for medical appointments, and so on.

Uplifting others has helped him to keep his own spirits high, and he believes that a bit of escapism can help people to feel happy, at least temporarily, no matter what's happening in their lives. He also feels it's important to speak openly about our struggles and mental health.

As difficult as lockdown has been, Aled doesn't want things to go 'back to normal', or rather, to the way they were beforehand. These times have restored his faith in people, and proved to him that humans are not the destructive race that is sometimes portrayed. He hopes that the new connections and friendships people have made will stand the test of time and leave a lasting legacy.

The world needs more of us to step up and start demonstrating our superpowers right now. Thank you Aled, for paving the way!

43
Marcuss Tisson

Marcuss Tisson is a comedian and teaching assistant from London's East End, who moved to Portsmouth at the start of 2020.

When the lockdown was first announced, his girlfriend Sandy Hunt encouraged him to arrange a socially distanced street party one Sunday with dancing and Bingo, having seen another entertainer featured on the news doing something similar. Marcuss had always loved bringing people together to meet others and have a good time, and so he agreed to the idea. Very soon he'd dropped 42 notices through his neighbours' doors to gauge interest.

The response was good, and on the day of the party, lots of people came out to enjoy the fun. The event proved so popular in lifting everyone's spirits that people began asking "When's the next one?", hence Sunday afternoon entertainment became a weekly feature! Almost everyone in the road is now on first name terms as a result, and Marcuss has been inundated with thanks, bottles of wine, raffle prizes, and other gifts.

One family in particular benefited more than most. Following an horrific car accident a few years previously, Shelley Page and her family had ceased to function properly due to post-traumatic stress and a serious head injury, and they'd became semi-reclusive. The street parties brought Shelley and her son Tyler out into the community again, where they were able to enjoy the music, dancing and games. This helped to build their confidence and social comfort levels again, and it was truly a transformative experience that they'll always be grateful for. Shelley's full story can be found later in the book.

Marcuss has a special interest in mental well-being, as both his parents suffered from mental ill-health. He set up support campaign 'Don't Suffer in Silence' after his mother Margaret died by suicide in 2016.

The family hadn't been aware of her battles with depression, and so Marcuss has campaigned ever since to remove the stigma that stops people from speaking up about mental ill-health. Older members of the community, who might have been raised to 'sweep things under the carpet' and not discuss their struggles, are likely to be at higher risk.

Marcuss has arranged mental health 'Walk 'n' Talk' events in the past, along with celebrity sponsored 'Stand up for Mental Health' comedy nights and galas to raise awareness and get people talking and laughing. He's looking forward to organising more of these events once it's safe for large groups of people to gather together again.

Marcuss and Sandy would like to thank the residents of Burleigh Road for making Sunday afternoons so much fun for everyone, and for all of their donations.

Many thanks to you both, for making so much possible for your neighbours this year.

Hannah Pilcher

Agency nursery worker Hannah Pilcher has had a life-long love of dinosaurs. One day during week two of lockdown, with time on her hands, and as part of her hour-a-day's exercise, she decided to pay a socially distanced visit to her friend Holly, and Holly's little boy Owen.

Nothing unusual about that, you might think, except for the fact that Hannah was dressed in an inflatable dinosaur costume that friends had previously encouraged her to buy online.

Hannah had thought initially that she'd use the costume to create some videos to entertain children during lockdown on social media platform *TikTok*, but her initial venture (filmed by her partner Stephen Woodford – a full-time *YouTuber*) got such a great response that she decided to venture out and about in the Portsmouth area in the costume too.

A dedicated Facebook page was created, the posts went viral, and thus, 'Hannahsaurus Rex' was born!

Hannah kept her Facebook page updated with news about when and where she was going to be, and people would come out of their homes with their children at those times, clapping, waving and cheering at the sight of the hilarious, waddling dinosaur

Very quickly, the press caught on, and the image of Hannah waddling through the streets of Portsmouth was broadcast across the region, via *BBC South Today* local news.

Hannah kept her *Facebook* page updated with news about when and where she was going to be, and people would come out of their homes with their children at those times, clapping, waving and cheering at the sight of the hilarious, waddling dinosaur. She was never sure who seemed to enjoy the sight more – the adults or the children!

By late summer, Hannah decided it was time to hang up her costume, and thus, *Hannahsaurus* was retired. However, she will remain a 'Legend of Lockdown' in our memories for years and decades to come.

Thank you for doing your bit to keep spirits up over lockdown, Hannah, and whatever happens in the future, keep shining your quirky, beautiful light for all to see!

45

Sally Turner

Sally Turner is a hula hoop teacher and hoop maker who moved into her home in Southsea in 2018 with her husband and two little girls.

Hula hooping is a joyful activity that delivers many benefits, including toning core muscles, strengthening the heart and lungs, and reducing body fat. The best bit is that it's fun!

Summertime usually involves Sally attending various summer fayres and festivals, giving demonstrations and running hula hoop classes. However, all of these events were cancelled due to the virus, and unusually, she found herself with time on her hands.

With the *75th anniversary of VE Day* looming, Sally waited a while to see if any of the more established residents of her road would suggest a street party. When nobody did, she decided to see if she could organise one herself, dropping leaflets, invitations, song-sheets and a DIY bunting set through all the doors, asking people to let her know if they were interested.

Many of the neighbours got in touch, and before long, decorations were up, ready for the big event.

On the day, everyone gathered outside of their homes, and Sally put up loud speakers to pipe out 1940s music, generating a wonderful, nostalgic atmosphere. They had afternoon tea, chatted, sang, danced and had a fabulous time – many of them getting to know people in their road properly for the first time.

Sally had promised a 'Special Guest Appearance' for the late afternoon, and at the chosen moment, formed a procession down the road, hula-hooping with her girls Violet (seven) and Olive (four) either side of her, dressed as the *Red Arrows* and doing an acrobatic display!

Celebrations went on until late in the evening, and Sally has since organised more doorstep events for the residents, including Bingo evenings and a quiz night. She's received many gifts and messages of thanks from neighbours young and old, who've told her the events made a big difference to them, and help them to feel less alone.

One neighbour gave her a photograph of their road that was taken on *VE day* itself (in 1945). It transpired that at that time, Sally's home was owned by a Mr & Mrs Hooper – a funny co-incidence given the hula-hoop connection.

Thank you Sally, for bringing your unique brand of fun and fabulousness to the world!

- 103 -

46

Simon Cattermole

Simon Cattermole is a teacher from Havant, with a passion for music and community.

When the virus broke out in the UK, he wasted no time in knocking on neighbours' door to offer his help, promoting his 'Pook Lane Patch' community *Facebook* page as a way of keeping the community up to date with events and in touch with each other.

Through this community page, Simon organised regular food collections for local food banks, by leaving a box outside his home for neighbours to donate items. He also organised a *VE Day* celebration for his road.

Perhaps the most popular thing he did was a weekly Saturday tea-time folk music performance for his neighbours. These started on the second occasion of the Thursday night 'Clap for our Carers', when Simon felt inspired to get out his guitar and sing *Somewhere Over the Rainbow*.

> *Perhaps the most popular thing he did was a weekly Saturday tea-time folk music performance for his neighbours.*

This went on to become #songsfromyourfrontporch – an initiative that helped to bring the people from neighbouring streets together (socially distanced, of course). Neighbours started talking to each other for the first time in some cases, and one resident who'd lived in the road for over twenty years said there had never been anything like it before. Even those unable to leave their homes commented on how pleasing and uplifting it was to have the music bringing people together.

Prior to this, Simon had been saddened to notice music and the Arts suffering in the area, so he was cheered to note the upsurge in creativity that was a happy by-product of the lockdown period.

Simon has recently written a lockdown song, and will be recording it shortly.

How exciting! We can't wait to hear it, Simon.

47

Ian Thomas

Ian Thomas from Southsea is a former musician from the *Royal Marines Band Service*. He joined the *Royal Marines Cadets* as a young boy, and served there for around nine years before entering the *Band Service* at the age of 17, where he stayed for 18 years.

As part of his basic training, Ian, who already played the flute and saxophone, had to learn another instrument, and he chose the violin. Musicians in the service have dual roles, and Ian found himself deployed to places like Iraq, Afghanistan and Kosovo as part of the *Medical Squadron*. It was a memorable time of his life, and a world away from the specialist carpet cleaning business '1st Impressions' that he runs today.

When the lockdown was announced, Ian, who owns a van, volunteered to shop for a number of people he knew who were shielding. He would do the shopping, deliver it and check on their wellbeing. This kept him busy at a time when his business had gone quiet, and as the weeks went by, he noticed a deterioration in some of the people he was shopping for, as the isolation took its toll. Where possible he would stay and chat for a while, knowing that he might be the only person they spoke to that day, and understanding the human need for talking and connection.

A few weeks into lockdown, when the 'Clap for our Carers' movement began on Thursday evenings, Ian's lodger, Ray, suggested that Ian get out his saxophone the following week, and play a few numbers for the neighbours. Ian agreed, and the session the following week went down a storm, with lots of lovely feedback and requests for a repeat the following week.

From that point on, the sessions became a weekly feature, with Ray acting as the PR person and Ian's partner Lisa staging the front of the house with NHS themed teddy bears and rainbows. The weekly entertainment continued right up until the clapping movement was brought to an end.

Ian entertained his street and other nearby neighbours with music of all kinds – always starting with the classic 'Somewhere Over the Rainbow', and then moving on to different genres, requests and themes. Some of the neighbours would dress up to tie in with the themes, variously in sombreros, Pink Panther costumes, and so on! He would generally play for around 25 minutes, and then people would stay around afterwards for a drink and a chat.

Music is something of a business side line for Ian, who has a contract with the *Warner Leisure* hotel group to play in their restaurants, and also offers background music for people's special occasions. During lockdown he performed in someone's garden for their 50th birthday party, and loves to bring his own brand of joy and energy to events.

Bravo, Ian! We hope you'll enjoy bringing the music to happy events and appreciative audiences for many years to come.

CREATIVITY STORIES

People are inherently creative, but we don't always realise that we are. Whilst we're good at nurturing creativity in our younger children, particularly in our nursery and infant schools, the focus tends to shift through junior and senior school, and by the time we reach adulthood, our natural creativity has often become dormant.

Lockdown left many of us with time on our hands and not much (after an initial spring-cleaning, organising and maintenance drive!) to do. The passive activities that many of us had become accustomed to filling our spare time with felt unfulfilling after a while, and we began looking for more creative, productive things to do.

There was an explosion of creativity, not just from the school-aged children who were brightening up the country with their colourful rainbow drawings and paintings, but from adults alike. Creative activities of all kinds were taking place, as we put our hands to good use and got crafty with writing, drawing and painting, photography, crafting, home cooking/baking, making music, crafting things from wood and clay, gardening (including 'growing your own'), flower arranging, knitting and sewing to furniture upcycling – the list goes on. And it felt good! Many of us had forgotten the benefits that expressing our creativity can bring; the fun we can have, the reduction in stress and anxiety we can experience (busy hands, quiet mind), and the sense of accomplishment and pride we can experience when we stand back and look at what we've produced or achieved.

There were stories in the media of care homes playing 'doorway bingo' with residents seated in the doorways of their rooms, facing out into the corridors where someone called the numbers. Later on, when restrictions began to lift and weather allowed, some care home residents enjoyed garden concerts.

The popularity of these activities and hobbies, which were commonplace at one time, had waned over the years. Whilst we'd begun to see a resurgence in activities like baking, sewing and crafting before the lockdown, thanks to a few popular television programmes, it probably wasn't until life slowed down during the pandemic, that creativity truly went 'viral'.

Our creativity went beyond arts and crafts, though, and crossed over into our thinking and imagination, ideas and solutions. From the businesses that were forced into thinking very creatively in order to adapt and survive, to the leaders who are now planning how we can create a better, safer world in the wake of everything that's happened, there's no doubt that the thinking of the past is not going to sustain us in the future.

Our aptitude for creativity, imagination, innovation, empathy, emotional intelligence, and our thinking skills, are what differentiates us from machines and robots. These are the skills and abilities that enrich our world, and that we need to nurture and develop in ourselves and our children.

Pretty soon technology will be doing the rest for us, and that's ok. We can't compete with machines and robots in some tasks, but we can stick to what we're best at – being caring, creative and amazing human beings!

48 Carrie Swinburne

Artist Carrie Swinburne was raised with the principle of giving to others. Prior to the lockdown, she'd raised over £500 for *Samaritans* through her workshops, and the sale of her art; however, her work as a volunteer at *Samaritans'* charity shop 'Sam's Place' in Southsea came to an end when the shop had to close, leaving her with spare time.

The following list details just some of the projects she kept herself busy with:

- As someone who used to make and do lots of different things with her children when they were small, Carrie decided to help those who were furloughed at home with their children. She devised the character 'Gorgeous Gloria the Glamorous Glue Queen', and dressed up in a glitzy, crazy outfit with lots of makeup, demonstrating various craft projects on video, via her *Facebook* page 'Floramora of Southsea'.
- She made NHS bunting and teddy bears to go in people's windows.
- She raised £700 for a friend who's an A&E nurse at *Queen Alexandra Hospital* in Cosham, who'd advised they were struggling for protective goggles. She did this by painting and selling 8-inch canvasses with various "Stay safe", and "Stay at home" messages – eventually running out of canvasses.
- When the '2.6 challenge' was on (an alternative to the marathon, which had to be cancelled), Carrie and her husband, Patrick, completed 2.6 miles in full *Morris Dancing* kit, with Patrick dancing and Carrie playing the melodeon! This raised £1,345 for *The Rowans Hospice*.
- She painted and donated a picture for *The Rowans Hospice' Tokens of Care* project. The design was turned into a *Tokens of Care* card.
- She painted and donated a picture of her local nursing home, where staff and residents had enjoyed a singalong during lockdown to "What a Wonderful World". It was a picture of the home with a rainbow over the top and the words "What a Wonderful World" within the rainbow. The nursing home later became Carrie's inspiration for a picture she created for an *Arts Council* funded 'Pause, Reflect, Create' project.
- She dropped free art around the Portsmouth & Southsea areas, as part of *#FreeArtFriday*, leaving it on benches in public areas where people could find it and take it home.

One of Carrie's favourites projects ever was painting the lobby of *Trinity Methodist Church* on Albert Road, Southsea, along with some artist friends.

Like her character Gloria, Carrie is a gorgeous and glamorous example of kindness and creativity! She shares a gallery in the *Hotwalls Studios* in Old Portsmouth, where you can see many examples of her cheerful and colourful work.

49

Piers Clouting & James Goddard

Piers Clouting, from Emsworth, was a 15-year-old schoolboy studying for his GCSEs when the country went into lockdown in March 2020. School was out early for those in their final year, as they were advised that they wouldn't be sitting exams, and would instead be granted predicted grades.

This left many with time on their hands, and Piers – a talented musician and songwriter – decided to get creative online with his friend James Goddard, with whom he'd played in bands since they were both 11. Piers was given his first guitar at the age of eight, and now plays lead guitar, rhythm guitar and bass, as well as being a great singer. James is an accomplished drummer and pianist, and loves the production side of things.

Piers' mum Claire lent him the money to buy a special laptop that enables music production, plus a microphone and some audio equipment. He and James, who'd been producing music for a couple of years, began to play around with ideas.

One day whilst on *FaceTime* together, Piers randomly recalled a melody he'd recorded a year previously. The pair then added a complimentary melody line, chords, a bass line, and finally some lyrics. Together they'd co-written a song that they later named 'Paper Kites'.

The creation of the main body of the song was relatively quick in comparison to the time spent afterward in production. This was a long and painstaking process which involved layers and layers of sound, with the addition of vocals, drums, synthesisers and arpeggios, as well as unique effects to give the song a full and professional sound. In the final stages, James mixed and mastered the track many times before they agreed on a version they were happy with.

After much discussion about what their new band name should be, they decided on 'Loose Change'. Piers designed and drew the cover art for the track, which was later painted by his sister Elizabeth. His mum Claire designed the eye-catching 'Paper Kites' logo.

The boys sought the help of music coach Immy Sleep from *Ovation Music* (a Chichester based charity offering opportunities for young musicians in the area) to get the song released. On 24th July the song went live across *Spotify*, *Apple Music*, *YouTube* and *Deezer*, and had racked up over 8000 streams across 59 different countries at the time of writing. www.youtube.com/watch?v=Th4cYE9notA

Whilst many young people found lockdown to be a difficult time, Piers was thankful for the opportunity it gave James and himself to fulfil a dream that might not otherwise have happened. They're now working on their second song, and looking forward to a new chapter in their lives as they begin college.

The future is looking very bright for this productive and creative duo. Best wishes, Piers and James. We look forward to watching your stars ascend!

50

Kelvin Uchemefune

Kelvin Uchemefune is a personal development coach and leadership trainer who lives in Portchester.

At the start of 2020 he began to feel that it was time for him to extend his influence, in order to reach people that he wouldn't ordinarily meet face to face. His mind went back to the book he'd attempted to write in 2018. At the time, Kelvin had managed to write a manuscript of 10,000 words. However, when he sent the first draft to a few trusted parties for their opinions, the feedback he received wasn't very encouraging. At that point he put the project aside, and almost gave up on the idea.

In April, when the country had gone into lockdown, Kelvin's business partner Mark Legg asked him if he'd ever thought about writing a book. Kelvin sighed, and shared the story of his earlier perceived failure, adding that publishing a book was still one of his goals.

Mark had written a book himself, and was eager to share some ideas. Mark's input, along with a famous quote from *Albert Einstein*: "In the middle of difficulty lies opportunity", spurred Kelvin on to pick up his manuscript and begin to write again.

He wasn't sure where the energy was coming from, but felt so motivated that within a week he'd written an additional 17,000 words. It was like a fire had been lit beneath him, fueling his dream.

Once he'd finished, he sent the manuscript off for proof-reading and editing, and on 30th May, published his first book: 'Revive - Six Steps to Rebooting Your Life' on *Amazon*.

The book conveys that whilst we don't always understand the lessons that life gives us, with the right strategies, and by holding onto hope without giving up, we can navigate even difficult waters and uncover the hidden opportunities. Kelvin is a living example of this message.

The lockdown period provided Kelvin with a wonderful opportunity to finish and publish his book. He is grateful for the unwavering support of his family, as well as the gift of time that lockdown gave him.

51
Emma Paxton

Prior to the lockdown, most of Gosport-based illustrator and graphic recorder Emma Paxton's work came from physically attending live conferences and events, capturing the key messages in visual format to be enjoyed and remembered thereafter.

When the "Stay at home" message was first announced and all public events were cancelled, Emma was left with a largely clear diary, and plenty of free time.

One day, whilst attending an online networking meeting where group members were discussing what they were doing to stay well and make the best of their time in isolation, Emma captured the information in an illustration entitled 'This Won't Last Forever', and posted it to her *Twitter* account.

The image went viral overnight, with 1000s of people and organisations liking and sharing it. This prompted Emma to post it across other platforms, and thus began two weeks of correspondence with people from all over the world, asking if they could use it for a variety of purposes.

Emma created an outline version for colouring in, which was well received by schools and parents schooling their children from home. She also created additional free printable resources, including online meeting cards and a bingo game, and made them available on her website, www.imagistic.co.uk.

The feedback she received as a result of these things was uplifting, with people referring to "...your delightful drawing", "...wonderful, heart-warming poster", "...cheery little sketches", "...filled with hope and great ideas to enhance wellness and quality time with family members".

An unexpected bonus from this worldwide exposure was being commissioned to do a number of paid jobs, working remotely for organisations in countries that Emma would never normally get to work in, and connecting with people she wouldn't usually have the opportunity to meet.

Lockdown taught businesses and organisations everywhere that you don't always have to gather people together in person, and it forced people to become more visual when presenting information.

Whilst Emma is looking forward to drawing in the live arena again, she's enjoyed the freedom that working from home as brought her, and hopes to achieve a greater balance of both in the future.

All the best, Emma!

52
Jen Evison

Jen Evison is a self-taught artist with seven years' teaching experience, who now runs short creative courses from her arts and crafts studio at *Priddy's Hard*, overlooking the water.

The studio is housed in a 300-year-old building that was originally coastguards' cottages. Jen has rented an upstairs unit there since March 2019, where she makes beautiful floral arrangements, cakes, gifts, and runs creative workshops of all kinds.

Jen's plans to open a small shop in a downstairs unit in early 2020 were de-railed by the virus. She lost all momentum at this point, and found the early days of lockdown extremely hard – especially has she'd been running at such a busy pace beforehand. Lockdown forced her to take a step back – to appreciate her flowering garden, and spend time with her children. As difficult as it was, she learned to surrender control and go with the flow.

At the beginning of the year, Jen had become involved with a number of charities and causes in Uganda, through social media. She explained, "It began with buying a talented young fashion designer a sewing machine so that he could sew his amazing creations a little quicker. Over lockdown the challenges many Ugandans have faced is devastating. People lost livelihoods and homes due to Covid restrictions. Food prices skyrocketed, and people were genuinely suffering.

The needs were endless, but one particular group stood out the most for me. Single mothers, trying to keep a roof over their heads and care for their children at the same time. Helping women secure little businesses became a need I could help to meet, and for just a few pounds, some of these ladies can regain their independence and confidence, as they provide for their families.

Having extra time during lockdown made me realise what I had in my life. A fulfilling business, a wonderful family around me, and the freedom to express my creativity in safety. So many women don't have this! Helping other women fulfil their potential has become so important to me."

From this, Jen has built up a network of incredible people in the UK and Uganda, and she and her team have big plans to build a women's refuge and centre of vocational training in Kampala next year.

Jen's shop, 'Jen Creates... Unique Gifts', was eventually able to open at the beginning of July. Feedback for this Aladdin's cave of crafts and unique, ethical gifts has been wonderful, and both Jen and the shop are rapidly building a community of raving fans.

Things don't always go to plan, or happen within our desired timelines. Sometimes, life throws us curveballs that can delay and derail us, and it can feel frustrating and demoralising. Letting go and allowing things to unfold in their own time this year has enabled Jen to not only deal with the curveball of *Covid-19*, but to smash it out of the park.

Loving your work, Jen, and wishing you all the best for your development projects in Kampala!

53

Michael Richardson

Michael is a student from Milton who first discovered a love for art whilst at pre-school. It took an art teacher in secondary school, however, to recognise and nurture Michael's talent, and to teach him the fundamental elements and principles of art, until he grew in skills and confidence.

Michael is dyslexic, and found it difficult to make friends whilst at school. He spent quite a lot of time on his own, and channelled his time and energy into painting as a way to relax and feel happier.

Michael sees the world in bright colours, and loves to capture the colours that he sees in nature – particularly in the warmer months. His paternal grandfather lives in the countryside, and used to take him and his twin sister out for nature walks when they were younger. Michael loved to sketch pictures of the landscape during these walks, and would later turn the sketches into paintings.

He believes he may have inherited his artistic flair from his maternal grandfather, who used to design sets and costumes for the theatre at the *National Museum of the Royal Navy* in *Portsmouth's Historic Dockyard*, many years ago.

Michael particularly loves painting pictures of Portsmouth's landmarks, as he was born in the city and loves its rich history and colours. He had a break from painting whilst completing his studies prior to the lockdown, but after spending some time doing gardening work at home, felt inspired to pick up his paintbrush again when all the spring colours starting bursting into life. He has hardly stopped painting since.

After posting a picture of one of his paintings on the 'Keep Milton Green' Facebook page, Michael received great feedback and lots of encouragement to start a Facebook page www.facebook.com/portsmouthart/). He hopes to make a career or side line out of his artwork.

Michael has made a lot of friends within the art community, and has a wonderful philosophy on life, always looking to see the good in people. He walks away from trouble, believing there are better things to do than hate one another, and stays away from anything that doesn't feel good.

He's looking forward to getting back on his career path again once things settle down, and hopes that all the countries of the world will come together to make sure that nothing like the pandemic can ever happen again.

We'll second that, Michael!

TRANSFORMATION STORIES

The virus, and subsequent lockdown, inspired transformations of all kinds.

In the early days, many of us found ourselves cleaning and clearing our homes, lofts, garages, gardens, and businesses. With time on our hands and spring in the air, we made the most of the opportunity to tackle all the jobs we'd often wished we had the time to do, but rarely got around to.

We were getting our homes and our lives in order – de-cluttering and organising like never before. Perhaps it was giving us a sense of control and order in a world where so much seemed to be happening outside of our influence. Whatever was driving it, our homes and vehicles were, in many cases, gleaming, and our gardens were blossoming. It seemed that the world itself had transformed, as nature blossomed and the landscape flourished.

The DIY and hardware stores (considered essential retailers) did a roaring trade, as people set about transforming their homes and gardens. Waste recycling centres and charity shops were closed, resulting in a 300% increase in fly tipping in some rural communities, as the less conscientious sought to dispose of their junk.

A massive digital transformation took place, as businesses and organisations were forced to quickly adopt online technology in order to keep their operations running. The 'burning bridge' of Covid had accomplished in a few weeks what many projects and programmes had been working to achieve over years.

We transformed our work and travel habits, as well as the way we socialised, shopped, holidayed, ate, exercised, and lived. Some people gained weight during lockdown, and others took the opportunity to lose weight, get fit and transform their bodies.

Some people took up meditation practises; others made big changes in their working hours, relationships, living arrangements, and so on. Some felt as though they'd undergone transformation at a deeper, more personal level, and that they were no longer the same people that they'd been, prior to the lockdown. We'd had the time to reflect on our lives and consider what was serving us, and what wasn't. Our priorities had changed. Some of the things that had once seemed important, no longer held the same significance.

Many had sensed (and astrologically, it was 'written in the stars') that 2020 was going to be a transformational year; yet very few imagined that it would be quite as transformational as it turned out to be!

54

Jane Cooke

Jane Cooke is a stylist, coach, mentor and founder of the Free-Range Women in Business network. Life had been extremely busy for a number of years prior to lockdown, with Jane latterly juggling two networking groups, her coaching and mentoring work, and a regular programme of public workshops.

Having an underlying health condition, Jane was advised to self-isolate for 12 weeks at the start of lockdown – a situation she did not relish, as an extroverted and highly social person.

When Jane's son James became seriously unwell in February and had to go into hospital, Jane and her husband Ian cut short their holiday in South Africa to return to the UK. The following six months or so involved a huge amount of worry and uncertainty, as James underwent tests, ongoing treatment, and had further blips and scares along the journey.

Grounded at home, concerned about her son, unable to see her daughter, and with most of her work suspended, Jane decided she needed a focus to keep her busy and distracted. She designed a programme of home organising and redecoration that would see Ian and herself through the lockdown period.

Thus followed months of hard but rewarding work in their home and garden, transforming both, and giving Jane ample opportunity to reflect on life and her business. During this time she found her priorities became clearer, and she was able to plan for a future which would bring greater balance.

Jane was able to continue the health and fitness regime she'd started at the beginning of the year, managing to lose an extra stone in weight which had been bothering her for a while.

Throughout the period, Jane kept in touch with members of her two women's networking groups, moving the meetings online via *Zoom* and making them free of charge, as many members had lost their business income. Later on, when restrictions began to lift (and when the weather allowed), Jane arranged socially distanced small group coffee gatherings in her garden. Having been self-employed since she was in her 20s, Jane knows how vital community, connection and support is for small business owners, and it's not an exaggeration to say that those meetings provided a lifeline to members at a time when many were feeling frightened, confused, and in some cases, alone.

As the year draws on, Jane is looking forward to designing some new home interiors workshops, and hopes it won't be too long before larger groups can gather together again. With a home as stylish and beautiful as hers, we know those workshops are bound to be a hit. 2020 might not have a been how Jane and Ian had envisaged it, but they made the most of the time they were given, and are now enjoying the fruits of their labour.

Great work, Team Cooke!

55

Marie Barnatt & Darren Mead

Marie Barnatt is an antenatal teacher for the *National Childbirth Trust* (NCT), and also runs dog grooming service 'Paws R Purrfect' from her home in Fareham.

When the lockdown was first announced, the NCT acted with lightning speed to move face-to-face ante-natal classes online. Instructors had to quickly familiarise themselves with the *Zoom* platform, and also prepare slides and adapt materials for the new way of working. The online format proved extremely popular with parents-to-be, and classes throughout July and August were fully booked.

Dog grooming, like hairdressing, wasn't possible for the first couple of months of lockdown, and dogs everywhere (like their humans) grew a little shaggy!

With time on their hands, Marie and her partner Darren (a former landscape gardener) decided to turn their energy and creativity into transforming their garden, with a bit of help from Marie's sons. Darren ordered all of the materials, and they got to work. Three days later he received a call to say it was OK for him to return to work, and so he ended up doing the landscaping in his evenings and weekends, not taking a day off for three months.

Flowerbeds were constructed, railway sleeper borders built, a patio was laid, and the lawn was lifted and re-turfed, amongst other jobs. Marie and Darren's planning application for a summer house to complete the works, stalled in June; however, after a five-month wait, they were thrilled to receive the go-ahead.

Marie's plans for her 50th birthday celebration in March had to be postponed, but she knows that the garden she'll be welcoming her friends to next year will be party-perfect!

Life is often very busy, and it can be hard to find the time and energy to do the DIY jobs and projects that we say we'd like to do someday. Marie and Darren have worked extremely hard to create a beautiful and thriving garden that they can finally enjoy and relax in – a living legacy of the coronavirus pandemic!

Wishing you many happy garden gatherings in the years to come!

56

Jeannette Jones

Jeannette Jones, of eco household products company 'Any Green Will Do' (a distributor for *Wikaniko*) is a grandma on a mission to transform our cleaning habits!

During the lockdown, she helped the cleaning revolution along by going mobile with her business, delivering eco-cleaning and skin-care refills to households along the south coast. In fact, she was busier than ever during this time, and she believes that habits are finally beginning to change as people become more conscious of the human impact on the environment.

Jeannette started her company when her grand-daughter Miya came along, to do her bit to safeguard the environment. "I wondered what animals would be around for Miya to see when she got older", Jeannette said. "It seems like an overwhelming task to save the world, but after discovering *Wikaniko's* products, I realised quickly that we don't have to try and do it all ourselves! If each of us took a few simple steps every day it would make a difference, create a few ripples and save us a bit of money, too. Little things like swapping from liquid soap to bars, or from washing powder and pods to an eco-laundry egg".

Jeannette's motto is

"It doesn't have to cost the earth to save the Earth."

57 Shelley Page & Family

Shelley Page is a mum of three and a full-time carer to her two autistic sons and disabled father. In 2016, her father, her eldest son Tyler and a family friend were involved in an horrific road traffic accident where the car was effectively sliced in half by a lorry. Tragically, their family friend died.

Tyler sustained a serious head injury, and Shelley's father (diagnosed the previous year with Guillain-Barré Syndrome) sustained injuries that rendered him more severely disabled. They had been going on holiday, and the accident happened just 20 minutes from their intended destination.

The accident, following hot on the heels of a year in which Shelley had faced eviction from her home, and suffered a miscarriage all on the same day, was so traumatic that even though she hadn't been in the car personally, she suffered with *Post Traumatic Stress Disorder* (PTSD) following all of the repercussions. This led to her becoming afraid to leave her home, because she found that the sight of lorries, the sound of sirens and loud noises, and even the presence of police, security and emergency services triggered panic in her, leading to behavioural meltdown.

Tyler also struggled to recover after the accident, and became reclusive like his mother.

Life has involved many struggles and battles for Shelley, trying to raise her three children whilst struggling with her own well-being at times, and having to fight in the courts for recognition and support for her sons' learning disabilities. Having to subsequently fight annually to maintain the support they receive in school is an added distress she wishes she didn't have to face.

Shelley found that lockdown gave rise to more anxiety, where trips to the supermarket would trigger panic. When her neighbour, Marcuss Tisson, began running Sunday 'Bingo & Boogie' parties for the street where the family live, Shelley and Tyler felt hesitant at first to come out of their home and join in, but they were enthusiastically encouraged to do so by Marcuss, whose aim was to bring happiness and togetherness to everyone on the street. Tyler came out of his shell during these parties, thoroughly enjoying the music and dancing. The neighbours were very supportive, and interested in the family's story.

Shelley said "The day the crash happened, we stopped living as a family, but Marcuss has helped us to start living again. We love our Sundays now, and we're so thankful to him. It's not easy to live in our conditions, but somehow we get through it. Some days we wobble. Some days it's difficult to pick ourselves up off the floor and leave the house, but we keep going, with a little bit of help".

Tyler came out of his shell during these parties, thoroughly enjoying the music and dancing. The neighbours were very supportive, and interested in the family's story.

Shelley worries about the future of mental health for the country coming out of lockdown, with funding and support being so stretched. She believes the next pandemic could be one of mental ill-health. Indeed, the *Royal College of Psychiatrists* have said they fear a tsunami of mental health referrals when lockdown measures end.

Her message to anyone in a similar position to her own is not to give up asking and fighting for the help and support they need, and even if they're having the worst day, to just hold on. "It's ok not to be ok" she says. "You will get through it, if you ask for help".

Shelley dreams of one day returning to university, and finding work where she can support others experiencing poor mental health and learning disabilities.

Hold the vision, Shelley! With your tenacity, we feel confident that you can find a way to make this happen.

58

Panashe Paradza (Baby Panna)

Panashe Paradza, aka Baby Panna, is a 20-year-old rap artist and poet who first came to the UK from Zimbabwe at the age of four.

At the time, he could speak no English, and quickly found himself in a school where he was the only black child. He had to contend with the other children touching his hair, asking silly questions sometimes, and making jokes.

Communication in the early days was laboured and frustrating. He didn't know how to ask to go to the toilet, and would just get up and leave the classroom when he needed to. It was another two years before he could speak the language, and the experience was very isolating.

The family moved around quite a bit during Panashe's school days, and he attended three different primary schools and two senior schools. At the age of 10, he formed a band with some school friends where he played the guitar – not too well, by his own admission! However, the time in the band helped to build his confidence, and lay the foundations for what would follow.

Senior school proved more troublesome than primary school had been, as the silly questions and comments he'd experienced earlier made way for more overt racism. Panashe's experience of the inner-city school he'd gone to first was easier than the school he later moved to in the leafy suburb of Waterlooville, where he experienced more prejudice and nastiness.

Panashe's love of music and poetry flourished during his senior school years, and he found healing power and self-expression in rap. He would often dream up beats and melodies in his head, recording them secretly into his phone. This went on for around seven years before he told those around him what he'd been doing. Within six months of going public, he'd recorded and released his first mixtape, to encouraging critical acclaim.

The period of time leading up to the lockdown was a reflective one for Panashe. He'd withdrawn socially for a few weeks to examine and recalibrate the way he'd been living his life. He was beginning to feel ready to reintegrate again when Covid-19 hit, effectively extending his period of reflection and isolation.

He felt a healing of old wounds during this time, accompanied by a surge of creativity which saw him becoming more innovative in his music, developing and transforming as a person and an artist. By the end of it he was feeling more centred, having worked out how much of who he'd become was actually himself, and how much was externally influenced. He spent time and energy connecting more deeply with his family, and made some adjustments in his friendships.

We met Panashe at a *Black Lives Matter* demonstration on a sunny September afternoon in *Portsmouth's Guildhall Square* – the day after the start of the *George Floyd* murder trial in America. That incident, and its timing, had shaken the world, helping to highlight the wounds of racism and injustice that run deep throughout society, providing an opportunity for reflection, discussion, education, and healing. Panashe gave a powerful and emotive performance of his track, 'Golden', on the steps of the Guildhall, with lyrics customised for the event, sharing the story of his personal experiences.

Panashe's music isn't industry standard rap. It has an authenticity and power to it that marks him out as an original. It carries his own story, energy and vibe, and he doesn't try to be anything other than himself. His ambition is simply to be the best artist that he can be, and to help other people through his music.

Panashe would love for everyone to be able to discover and pursue their innate creative talents – to find their 'thing' and be given the opportunity to master it. Through his music and lyrics, he's helping to create a new world – a world where people aren't put into boxes; where children can grow up with the confidence to be themselves and follow their own paths, without allowing other people's opinions to define them. And he'll do it with his trademark flow and creativity – Baby Panna style!

59

Ceri Winfield

Ceri Winfield is a rehabilitation therapist and fitness enthusiast from Hill Head, who works with children who have disabilities.

Lockdown was a tough time for Ceri who, being self-employed, was very concerned about how she and her business would survive. The financial packages initially put in place to support businesses didn't include supporting limited companies operating from home premises, and she was worried.

The lockdown period started with Ceri breaking up with the boyfriend with whom she'd been living. Whilst it was her decision to end the relationship, and she knew that it was ultimately the right thing for both of them, it was difficult emotionally, and left Ceri on her own with her two little dogs.

It was Ceri's 30th birthday on 27th March – an event that, in any other circumstances, would have meant a celebration and gathering of friends. As the lockdown rules were at their tightest at that point and everyone was strictly observing the "Stay at home" directive, Ceri didn't see another person all day. In fact, there were periods during lockdown where she didn't see or speak to anyone face-to-face for days.

A month after her birthday, and completely out of the blue, one of Ceri's two little dogs, Trixie, passed away. The two of them had been inseparable since Ceri was 21, and were the best of buddies. Trixie had helped her through difficult times, and whilst she still had Tank (her other little dog), there was no-one to give her a hug.

Ceri had had a fairy-tale wedding at the age of 27. The couple were together for 5 years in total, but when the passion and excitement gave way to something more platonic, the relationship didn't survive. When her divorce papers came through during lockdown, it brought up residual sadness for dreams held and lost; however, Ceri was thankful for the lessons that her marriage and divorce had taught her.

Many of us are taught to look for happiness outside of ourselves – often from other people, and especially from our closest relationships. We're sold romantic dreams of meeting 'the one', and living happily ever after – not realising that happiness is an inside job, determined largely by how we see things and think about them. No-one else can give happiness to us – we have to generate it for ourselves through love – love of ourselves, love of others, and of doing what we love, following our authentic passions. Ceri decided that what she really needed was to get happy with herself, physically and emotionally. She'd been into fitness for some time, taking year-round early morning swims in the sea (banned in the early months of lockdown) as well as vigorously working out. She'd also been due to take part in an *Ironman triathlon* in July, but this was cancelled due to the virus.

Much of the exercising had been driven by Ceri's unhappiness with her size. With swimming and the Ironman off the cards, she decided that the only thing left to do was to focus on her eating. In early May she signed up for online weight-loss journey 'The 6 Pack Revolution' – a 75-day transformation programme covering nutrition, fitness and mindset, which helped Ceri to change how she sees things. She even decided to undergo counselling as a way of processing negative past events, to enable her to move forward into a more positive life.

Ceri's end goal is to find herself again – to enjoy living a positive and healthy lifestyle that she enjoys and that feels like a pleasure rather than a chore. She wants to feel proud of who she is – a successful person in her own right, who isn't defined by her relationship status, and doesn't need to be one half of a couple to feel that her life's worth living.

Ceri is a goal-oriented person who is now looking forward to new challenges, and helping as many children and families as possible through her work. Lockdown has undoubtedly been a difficult time for her, however the story isn't a sad one, but an inspiring story of empowerment and finding strength within. She has undoubtedly undergone a radical transformation from the inside-out, and is ready to step into the future with new-found confidence and determination.

Go Ceri!

MISCELLANEOUS STORIES

Whilst there were a number of clear themes that emerged during lockdown, there were inevitably some stories that fell outside of easy categorisation – hence the need for a 'Miscellaneous' section in this book.

Lockdown was a relatively quiet time for politics in the UK, with most of the news centring around the virus, and taking the focus off the Brexit negotiations. At the time of printing (November 2020) no deal had been agreed, with existing arrangements due to end on 1st January, 2021.

There were some themes from lockdown that aren't represented here in stories. For example, instances of family and domestic violence reportedly rose, along with relapses in drug and alcohol addiction and misuse. Samaritans reported that the virus was disproportionately affecting society's most vulnerable people, exacerbating some of the factors known to be related to suicide, such as financial difficulty, and poor mental health.

In compiling this book, we didn't consciously seek out, or avoid, stories of any kind. They came to us organically via our networks, and through social media. We noticed that most of the stories had a positive slant, and wondered why there was relatively little in the way of Covid-19 cases and deaths within these pages. Whilst it's probable that people are more likely to go public with stories of a positive nature than those of a not-so-positive nature, it's likely to be more representative of the fact that in any cross-section of 70 people in the south of England, few, if any, (at the time of publishing at least) would have been impacted by the virus personally.

Whilst lockdown was clearly a difficult time for many, and the loss of life was significant, there were a lot of positives, too. Maybe there are gifts to be found in all of life's experiences, and there's learning to be gleaned from every situation.

When pondering what to call this book, we played with lots of different words - stories of love, faith, hope, and so on. We had a sense that, despite the bumpy ride we were experiencing, everything was happening for the greater good, and it would all work out fine in the end.

This is where faith and hope come in. From our human perspective, we can't always see what good might come out of a seemingly cataclysmic event like this. We just need to hold on to a bit of faith and hope that it will all come good, and the story will have a happy ending.

We hope you'll enjoy the rest of these stories.

60

David & Gillian Prichard

Lockdown was a relaxing time for David and Gillian Prichard, who live in a village near Petersfield in Hampshire. David, a retired structural engineer who enjoys sculpting, and his wife Gillian, moved to the area from Surrey 22 years ago.

The spring and summer months in Hampshire during lockdown were glorious. David and Gillian's small, sheltered garden with views across the South Downs became their outdoor living space during this time, providing an area for alfresco meals, watching the garden birds raising their young, and observing the plants and shrubs coming into bloom.

As the warm, sunny days drew to a close, the couple delighted in the magnificent sunsets and red skies that would predict another fine day to come. The absence of aeroplanes in the skies, along with very little traffic on the roads and horse riders trotting through the picturesque village, gave them the feeling of village life as it would had been many years ago. The huge haymaking vehicles slowly making their way down the narrow high street were the only hint of industry; a reminder that it was 'business as usual' for the farms in the surrounding countryside.

David and Gillian, who normally look forward to a UK holiday during May, took many walks in the South Downs area instead, enjoying the distant views and abundant wild flowers. Although restricted from travelling, and therefore unable to visit their children and grandchildren, they were able to stay in touch with them by telephone and Zoom.

The couple feel fortunate that their experience of lockdown was a pleasant one, and appreciate that this wasn't the case for everyone. They are also very appreciative of the great kindness they received from the neighbours who helped them with shopping whilst they were shielding.

David and Gillian's prevailing memory from lockdown is of the peace they experienced when out on their walks, coupled with the vibrant conversations they exchanged with the people they met en route, which they found very uplifting.

They found that people in general seemed more inclined to engage in conversation with others during this time, and to connect at a deeper level than was customary. This helped to create a greater sense of community spirit, increasing feelings of happiness and well-being.

Many thanks for sharing your lockdown story, David and Gillian, and we wish you many more sunsets and fine days to come.

61
Ginny Downey & Pat Ralph

Ginny Downey's mum Pat Ralph was dreading her 90th birthday on 5th May, as she was having to isolate, and the family had had to postpone her big party at *The Queens Hotel* in Southsea.

The only person visiting Pat during this time was Ginny, at a distance, when she delivered her groceries.

Ginny and her husband, Bob, wanted to make the day as special as possible, given the difficult circumstances, and they arranged a number of lovely surprises for Pat, including the following:
- ordering the Victorian lamp post, from the family, that she'd always wanted for her garden;
- having some "Happy 90th Birthday Mum" t-shirts printed;
- ordering a cream tea, and decorating the table with banners and balloons;
- arranging for friends and relatives to drop by the doorstep with cards and presents, including some seahorse gifts (Pat loves to collect seahorses) and a painting;
- arranging video calls with family from further afield, where everyone sang *Happy Birthday*.

Pat had a wonderful day despite the restrictions, and thoroughly enjoyed being spoiled.

Her birthday party at *The Queens Hotel* was rescheduled to later in the year (and subsequently, again, to May 2021), giving Pat a second birthday celebration (rather like the Queen!).

She is now looking ahead ten years to celebrating her 100th birthday in 2030, at which time she hopes to book HMS Warrior for a party!

Many congratulations on such a milestone birthday, Pat, and well done Ginny for all your thoughtful planning, which helped to create such a special day for your mum, against the odds.

62

Chris Pink

Chris Pink is a vehicle leasing broker from Chichester. In 2015, after 20 years in the automotive industry, he set up his business 'Pinksauce' offering 'whole of market' vehicle leasing and subsidiary services.

When the country went into lockdown in March 2020, it provided Chris with a timely pause for thought. Going self-employed, and working from his beach-hut style garden office, had given him a better work/life balance and more time with his family, following years of zooming up and down the motorways, clocking up around 4,000 miles a month. A bonus was that it had also reduced his risk of death or injury – something he'd become very aware of, having witnessed road traffic accidents over the years, and observed some appalling risk-taking from other road users. There seemed to be so many stressed people rushing around from place to place at break-neck speed – presumably to avoid being late, or because they were on some kind of time bonus.

Sitting in his beach hut during lockdown one day, Chris realised that the only zooming he'd done for a while was attending online meetings and social gatherings on *Zoom*! He pondered whether the Covid-19 pandemic would turn out to be the catalyst that finally changed our unsustainable working and driving habits, reducing stress and benefitting us mentally, physically, environmentally and economically.

Chris had been talking to his childhood friend Dave around this time, about his general well-being. The two had known each other for nearly 40 years, and whilst banter had always been a theme within their friendship, Chris had learned how to listen at a deep level from sales training workshops he'd attended in the past. He had never forgotten the saying, "You have two ears and one mouth, so we should listen twice as much as we speak".

From the outside, Dave appeared happy and successful. He'd similarly been driving up and down the country for years, striving to meet challenging sales targets, up early, home late, taking calls (hands free) whilst trying to navigate to his destination, and spending precious little time with his family. Under the surface of 'keeping it all together' was a conscientious and caring man suffering from extreme stress.

Luckily Dave made the decision to seek help, but not before his thoughts had turned to whether he should drive his car off the road or jump in front of a train, because he didn't want to wake up the next day feeling the same way. It was difficult for Chris to hear this, and he wished that Dave had felt comfortable talking to him sooner.

The change in Dave whilst working remotely during lockdown, and being able to have a laugh again with his mates online, was great for Chris to see. Chris jokingly pointed out that, based on the advice he'd given him previously, he was driving one of the safest cars on the market, and his actions might not have succeeded!

He had never forgotten the saying, "We have two ears and one mouth, so we should listen twice as much as we speak".

Chris believes that if the pandemic will have encouraged individuals and organisations to reflect on, and re-evaluate, their habits and operating models, it will ultimately be good for both the people and the planet. Benefits will include helping to prevent burnout, reducing road rage, driver stress, accidents, traffic jams, fuel prices, and carbon footprint.

Whilst it might sound strange that a vehicle leasing broker would be encouraging people to drive less (after all, lower miles mean lower payments), Chris believes that honesty and integrity are the best strategy for long-term success in business.

His many satisfied customers agree!

63

Bill Moulsdale

The year brought mixed emotions for Bill Moulsdale – a resident of Port Solent who originates from Scotland.

Bill's older brother became very ill during lockdown, and passed away a short time later. As his brother lived in Scotland, Bill was unable to visit him in the later stages of his illness, or attend his funeral afterwards, due to travel restrictions.

Fortunately, Bill had managed to catch up with his brother during a trip South earlier in the year. At this meeting, his brother had shared the news that he was terminally ill with cancer, and had been given just a few months to live.

As someone who'd been diagnosed with cancer himself some seven years earlier, Bill had not expected to outlive his brother. It was a strange feeling knowing that his brother had gone, and not having had the chance to pay his last respects.

In fact, within the space of 12 months spanning 2019-2020, Bill lost five close family members, although not to Covid-19. It was a lot of loss to deal with over a relatively short space of time.

The human spirit is resilient, though, and Bill is strong. A positive and popular individual, he believes that, with due reverence, we shouldn't wallow for too long pondering life's sadness or losses. Lockdown gave him a push that he said he needed to make some changes in his life and to his business, 'Giant Leap Video & Photography'. He let go of his business premises at Lakeside, and set up a studio from his home, adopting a new business model. He's been surprisingly busy with work ever since.

Bill also used the lockdown period to clear and de-clutter an accumulation of life and business paperwork and junk that was no longer needed.

His next project is to tackle his garage, beyond which he is looking forward to chilling out with some time spent on the water – his true 'happy place'.

That sounds good to us, Bill!

64

Mandy Tourle

Mandy Tourle is a self-employed former solicitor and trust and estate practitioner who now specialises in helping older people and their families to deal with the paperwork that later life brings. She acts as a sounding board and adviser to her clients, enabling them to keep control of their affairs whilst making informed decisions, and providing them with peace of mind that everything's in place.

At the beginning of lockdown, those over the age of 70 were told to self-isolate, hence much of Mandy's work (usually done face to face, and requiring signatures) stopped overnight. It was a time of significant vulnerability for many, and some of Mandy's clients sadly passed away.

In January, one client who Mandy had known for four years, died very suddenly. His wife, who had *Alzheimer's* disease, was living in a care home, and his family were all living in Wales. The family instructed Mandy to organise his funeral, which she did. Then when Covid-19 hit, the gentleman's wife sadly died too. Having no family of her own, her executor was a friend of her deceased husband, and he asked Mandy to help with the funeral arrangements.

Knowing very little about this lady, Mandy had to go through all of her paperwork in order to piece together the story of her life. She found photographs and newspaper cuttings of the couple's wedding, and took note of the flowers the lady had held, duplicating these for the funeral. She spoke to a few of the lady's friends, and gathered stories. Mandy discovered that she'd been part of the *Royal Electrical & Mechanical Engineers* (REME) *Corps* during the war, and arranged for music by the REME military band to be played at the funeral.

Mandy has great respect for our older citizens, whom she finds to be strong, resilient and resourceful. They've generally been through wars and tough times, and know what it means to really struggle – to camp out in bunkers with no heating; to lose their homes; to go hungry. Our lives today in general (even during lockdown) are easy and luxurious by comparison, and we can often fail to value and appreciate the wisdom and life experience that our elders have to share.

On the day of the funeral, Mandy was the only person physically in attendance, with a further two being present via video link. Travel wasn't permitted at this stage, and so the lady's relatives in Wales were unable to attend. Whilst it was a strange and sad funeral, Mandy had made sure that it was as personal and beautiful a service as it could be, in the circumstances.

Even in the funerals held later in lockdown when more people were able to attend, things just weren't the same, with attendees being unable to console one another physically. There's nothing that says "I'm here for you" in quite the same way as a hug.

As well as arranging a number of funerals, Mandy made herself helpful to others locally and a bit further afield, doing shopping and running errands for those who couldn't get out, including her own family. Her mother, father and sister all live together and were shielding her dad, who has a suppressed immune system. Whilst it was hard for Mandy having to communicate with them on the door-step in the early days, she found that in a funny kind of way, lockdown brought them closer together. They were more supportive and appreciative of each other, and shared more laughs, more Facetime calls, and more great conversations than ever before.

Mandy and her family are now looking ahead and have started planning for the future. It might not have been the easiest of times, but they've found that lockdown delivered some wonderful benefits. They hope that the camaraderie, support and kindness that people everywhere have shown to one another will continue.

Thank you, Mandy, for all that you do to help people day to day, and particularly for venturing out of your usual remit during lockdown. Our world wouldn't be the same without the givers and the good souls that dedicate their time to helping others in whatever way is needed.

65 Francis Leonard (The Leonard Family)

When the country went into lockdown, Amy Leonard, from Clanfield in Portsmouth, went into hibernation. Mum of two, Amy, who was considered clinically vulnerable, was advised to shield. Her husband, Richard, worked from home, whilst the couple's two children, Francis (pictured) and Aidan, were home-schooled.

With the exception of two occasions where she sneaked out for a walk with the family, Amy was confined to her home for what she described as "12 glorious weeks". It fell to Richard to ensure that the family's dog, Nero, and their two children, were regularly exercised!

The early days of lockdown were challenging for Amy socially, as she could only speak to her mum and other people through the window. Fortunately, she lives on quite a busy road along which many of her friends regularly pass by, so she would wave at them when she could, and beckon them over for a chat.

Francis turned seven around the same time that the country went into lockdown, and was due to have a party with her friends on 23rd March. Unfortunately, the party had to be cancelled – a sad moment for Francis, but she was very mature about it, and understood the reasons.

Francis' brother Aidan, who was eight at the time, created a treasure hunt for Francis' birthday, with a map and clues as to whereabouts in the home and garden she could find her presents. The family made sure that Francis had a lovely day, despite missing out on her party. In fact, the family put a lot of creative energy into enjoying their time together in lockdown, and did all sorts of fun things to help the time go by pleasurably. This included:

- An Easter egg hunt involving an assault course in their kitchen/dining room, where the upturned table became a tunnel of balloons, and where wool was criss-crossed around chair legs for added difficulty and peril!
- Cooking as a family, including savoury dishes such as the children's favourite, lasagna, and lots of cake baking
- Camping out in a tent in the garden, when Nero was given special permission to sleep on Aidan's camp bed
- Online music and gym lessons
- A VE day home celebration where they baked scones and a Victoria sponge cake, and had an indoor picnic
- Home cinema nights, where Grandma would drop off sweets and popcorn, and they'd make and drink 'slushies'
- Board game afternoons, and family jigsaw puzzles
- Home haircuts, where Amy cut everyone's hair using clippers after watching tutorials on *YouTube*, and where Richard also cut Amy's hair with clippers!
- Homemade 'take-aways'
- Sleep-overs, where the children would take it in turns to 'sleep over' in their parents' room

- Teaching Francis to ride her new bike, and as restrictions began to ease, going on family bike rides
- Sea swimming at Lee-on-the-Solent for Granny's 70th birthday on 24th June
- A trip to 'secret island' at Langstone Harbour (a sandbank which appears when the tide goes out) for Aidan's nineth birthday in August, with Amy's parents, who have a sailing boat. Kayaking, and watching seals play in the harbour
- Park meet-ups with friends, and walks in the woods
- Adventure golf at *Chichester Golf Club*
- And far too much *Minecraft*!

After 12 weeks in isolation, Amy found it rather stressful acclimatising to the outside world. She'd become comfortable in her protective bubble, and felt nervous coming out of it and finding her way in the world again. The family had grown accustomed to the new way of shopping, whereas for Amy it was all new. She did adapt, though, and it's fair to say that the family had a blast, and have hundreds of fabulous photographs to remember the time by.

The early days of lockdown were challenging for Amy socially, as she could only speak to her mum and other people through the window.

Amy is really appreciative of the amazing time she had during lockdown with her husband and children – time that they'd have never had otherwise. It brought them all closer together as a family, and she'll always remember it as a lovely, happy time.

What a gorgeous story and example of how, with a bit of creative thinking and effort, we can turn the most difficult of times into something positive. Whatever 2021 brings for Francis' eighth birthday, in the immortal words of *Dame Vera Lynn*, we know that she'll "keep smiling through"!

...oosing Normandy
Le Havre
Bayeux
Caen
Saint Lô
Falaise
Calais
Dunkirk
Boulogne
BELGIUM
Abbeville
...ORMANDY
Vs
PAS DE CALAIS
Cons
Pros
Cons
TOP SECRET
NORMANDY
TOP SECRET
... Calais is a convenient stone's throw
Sir Bertram Ramsay
Sir Arthur Tedder

66

Victoria House - The D-Day Story

Victoria House is a duty manager at The D-Day Story in Southsea – a museum run by *Portsmouth City Council* that tells the story of *D-Day* and the *Battle of Normandy*. It's the story of the liberation of Europe from *Nazi Germany*, and is told in three parts (Preparation; *D-Day* and the *Battle of Normandy*; Legacy and the *Overlord Embroidery*), through the experiences, words and personal possessions of the men, women and children of the day.

Since opening its doors in May 2018, *The D-Day Story* has received excellent feedback, and been shortlisted for the prestigious *European Museum of the Year Award*, 2019.

When the country went into lockdown, the museum had to close its doors to visitors. *HIVE Portsmouth's Covid* response team took over one of the rooms, which became the base from which they co-ordinated support efforts across the city, in partnership with local charities and organisations.

From the outset, the *HIVE* team worked extremely hard, operating seven-day weeks before eventually dropping the weekends when things began to calm down. It was a hive of activity, with multiple meetings every day, and many people dropping off deliveries of protective equipment, food and donations.

Victoria was part of a team of museum staff who worked shifts, opening up the building for *HIVE* staff at 7:30 am, and closing up again at 5:30 pm. As well as conducting their essential health and safety checks, the museum team also answered all the *Visit Portsmouth* tourist information centres' phone and email enquiries, assisting with a mail-out of brochures, amongst other duties.

During this time, the team were encouraged to update their mandatory training, and also explore further training opportunities. Victoria noticed an online coaching & mentoring training course being advertised on the city council's intranet site. With her manager's approval, she signed up for the course and completed it over the next three months, fitting the work in around her other duties. This added an additional purpose to her role, and gave her a new set of skills that she hopes to put to good use in the near future.

Around mid-July, the *HIVE* team left, and the museum re-opened. They've been extremely busy ever since, with their new attraction – a huge, refurbished landing craft tank known as *LCT 7074* – drawing the crowds in. Whilst it's been quite difficult trying to manage everything safely, ensuring that everyone's observing distancing and hygiene rules, the team all pulled together and their new systems are working well.

Victoria is thankful that she had a positive experience of lockdown, when she knows this wasn't the case for everyone. Keeping herself busy, and taking the time to appreciate her surroundings, helped.

D-Day was a success because countries joined forces, and ordinary people pulled together to achieve an extraordinary result. We can achieve amazing things when we all work together to achieve a shared goal – even win the war against this virus.

67 William Plimmer

William (Will) Plimmer is a carpenter and joiner from Hampshire. He's also the proud father of Maxwell, his son and best friend. Lockdown for Will was a time of highs and lows, although thankfully, a few more of the highs. Will was self-employed, but had worked consistently for family-run construction business *RW Complete Ltd* in Funtington for nine years, and they'd always been very busy until Covid-19 hit, when they had to close their doors.

Will found himself at home, unable to qualify for the government's furlough scheme, and worried about money. He and his girlfriend Danielle had been due to purchase their first house together, and it looked as though plans might have to go on hold.

Will had previously set up a small workshop in one half of his mum and dad, Penny and John's, double garage. In fact, that part of the garage had been his parents' own workshop at one time – a photo-processing darkroom.

Being locked down, and with no work to occupy him, Will decided he would start making wooden planters. The weather was lovely, and it was the perfect time of year to start sowing vegetable seeds. He purchased a large amount of seeds, and these were planted and nurtured by Penny and John, whilst Will set about making the planters.

Soon afterwards, Will received a phone call from one of his business friends, asking him to quote for making a wardrobe. Thus, the next part of Will's lockdown journey began! Three wardrobes later, and having invested in his own set of quality tools (difficult financially, as he bought the best and most expensive), he's now running his own business – W Plimmer Design + Woodwork.

Fortunately for Will (but unfortunately for Penny and John!), he has now claimed the whole of the double garage as his workshop. Alas, Penny's pride and joy – a beautiful *Mazda MX-5 Mk1* – was destined for the driveway.

The Plimmers have always had a dog, and Molly, the family's black cocker spaniel, had a litter of puppies in May 2018. They decided to keep two of the puppies, giving one to Will – a loveable brown spaniel whom he named Aayla. Aayla became Will's second best-friend after Maxwell, and always wanted to be close to him, followed him (and Maxwell) around everywhere.

Will and Danielle would often walk their dogs together, and one of their favourite places to walk was along the disused railway line in the Meon Valley. One sunny day during lockdown, they decided to take a different turn than their normal one, not knowing that there was a country road below.

Aayla, being a spaniel, was always very busy, and loved to be outdoors. On this beautiful, sunny day, Aayla disappeared off down a bank, and then tragedy struck. She was hit by a van, and in that moment, it felt like Will's whole life fell apart. Danielle called Penny in a desperate state, not knowing what to do. Aayla very sadly passed away in Will's arms at only two years and 12 days old, and the whole family was devastated.

Will was beside himself, and there was nothing anyone could do, apart from comfort him. He was thankful at this time for the support he received from his friends and family, which helped to pull him through. The days after the incident passed by in a haze, but of course, life had to carry on.

Thanks to a government self-employment grant, Will was able to purchase a large and sophisticated, second-hand, multi-functional joinery machine – quite a lump of machinery, but a necessary buy, for the bespoke carpentry projects that were coming his way thick and fast.

> *Being locked down, and with no work to occupy him, Will decided he would start making wooden planters.*

The purchase of Will and Danielle's first home together eventually went through, and Will is now busier than ever, as the couple renovate the house together in their evenings and every other weekend. On alternate weekends, Will spends every second with his best buddy, Maxwell. He feels proud to have such a well-mannered, bright and fun-loving boy to call his son, and the time that they spend together is full of love and laughter.

Will & Danielle still have plenty to do in their house and Maxwell is becoming a dab hand with a paintbrush! Will, Danielle and Maxwell hope to be in their new house for Christmas 2020.

There's still a small, Aayla-shaped hole in Will's heart, but with all the love he has around him, it should heal nicely in time.

EPILOGUE

2020 will be a year that we never forget. From the bushfires, to Brexit, to political shenanigans across the pond, the one thing that seemed to eclipse it all (and the event we'll remember for all time) was the Covid-19 pandemic and subsequent lockdown.

At the time of publishing, the virus had affected 188 of the world's 195 countries, and numbers were still climbing in half of them following a 'second wave'. No one knows yet how the story will end, although hopes of a vaccine by Easter 2021 are being widely touted, and there are suggestions that the virus is becoming weaker.

It was a year that rocked and tested us – an historic moment in time, the likes of which few of us had ever experienced. Having our many freedoms curtailed was tough, and the isolation for many was hard to bear. We realised how much we need connection and community, and how vital it is to our well-being to talk and socialise, to laugh and exchange love.

The virus inspired us to look after ourselves, other people, and our planet much better than we'd been doing previously. As we changed our habits, the effects had rippled out and changed the world. We'd had space to breathe, and time to think. Our values had changed.

The opportunity is there for us now to hold onto these changes; to remember the lessons we've learnt, and to create better, more sustainable ways of living. However, it could also be very easy for us to fall back into old habits, if we don't consciously guard against it. Behaviour is habitual, and the path of least resistance is seductive. We'll need to think differently, feel differently, and behave differently, if we want to safeguard our quality of life and our future on the planet, going forwards. We'll need to think in terms of 'We', not 'I', understanding that we're all in the situation together, and that the way out of it will also be together, as a collective rather than a disparate bunch of individuals or countries.

Like a plastic snow-globe, we've been shaken up this year. Everything's been up in the air, and chaos and confusion have been all around us. The virus has been a wake-up call for humankind, and before things start to settle, we have an opportunity to start anew – to put all differences (perceived and otherwise) aside, and unite around a common goal – the goal of ensuring that all people and all life on the planet flourish forever.

As Her Majesty the Queen said in her address to the nation in the springtime, "We should take comfort that while we may have more still to endure, better days will return: we will be with our friends again; we will be with our families again; we will meet again". And hugs will prevail!

ACKNOWLEDGEMENTS

Our grateful thanks, first and foremost, to the amazing people whose stories we've shared here. We've been incredibly touched, inspired and uplifted by your stories, and it was a treat to speak with you all in the strange and disconcerting days of lockdown. We're still hoping to be able to hold a launch party at some stage, where we can bring you all together to meet one another in an afternoon or evening of celebration. Maybe we'll encourage a few of you to get up on stage and showcase your talents – hopefully with a few Portsmouth Distillery 'Quarantinis' on hand for extra cheer!

Many thanks also to our husbands and families for tolerating the disruption to normal life, even during evenings and weekends, when we would sometimes disappear to capture stories and take photos. We love you, and we're sorry!

This project was completed on a shoestring. As freelancers, work was thin on the ground for us both, and some months there was very little money coming in. Friends and relatives have helped us at various stages – sometimes for nothing, and sometimes at 'mates' rates'. It was a team effort, and we've been grateful to have you on our team.

Thankfully, our "Let's crack on, and worry about how we'll make it happen later" approach worked (phew!). We don't know for sure exactly what magic it is that seems to work behind the scenes at times to make things happen, but we're certainly grateful for it.

Deep gratitude to Penny's dad Terry Cattermole for his many hours of proof-reading, and suggested amendments. Many thanks also to Richard Pegg for the cover design, to Tricia Charles for the book's interior design, and to Adrian Aspinall for his help with marketing copy.

Extra special thanks to Ginny Downey for her enthusiastic cheerleading, liking and sharing on social media!

Finally, to you, the reader, for your investment in the book, from which a percentage of the profits will be donated to the charities and charitable organisations whose stories feature. Know that in buying this book, you have helped these organisations to continue the wonderful work that they do, day-in and day-out, even when there isn't a pandemic taking place!

Here's to YOU!

Caroline Martin with her partner, John, and her sons Finley and Charlie.

Photo taken by Penny, on one of her many bicycle jaunts through Horndean and Clanfield during the early lockdown period. This kept her very fit, and also cheered people up!

"A rainbow is a promise of sunshine after rain, of calm after storms, of joy after sadness, of peace after pain, of love after loss"